# ECONOMETRIC STUDY OF SPATIAL POPULATION MOBILITY IN INDIA

# Econometric Study of
# Spatial Population Mobility in India

A Study of Rajasthan

*By*
**Dr. Anju Kohli**

**ANMOL PUBLICATIONS PVT. LTD.**
**NEW DELHI - 110 002 (INDIA)**

**ANMOL PUBLICATIONS PVT. LTD.**
4374/4B, Ansari Road, Daryaganj
New Delhi - 110 002

*Econometric Study of Spatial Population Mobility in India*



First Edition, 2000

ISBN 81-261-0661-1

ICSSR Consultant: Dr. (Mrs.) S. Murthy

[The publication of this book is partially financed by the Indian Council of Social Science Research, New Delhi. However, the responsibility for the facts stated, conclusion reached etc., is entirely that of the Author and the ICSSR bears no responsibility for them.

PRINTED IN INDIA

Published by J.L. Kumar for Anmol Publications Pvt. Ltd., New Delhi - 110 002 and Printed at Mehra Offset Press, Delhi.

# *Contents*

# Preface

Inter-regional population movements have a long history and in the present day world, it is also a common phenomenon in the process of development. It has been able to create great interest among scholars from the various disciplines like demography, geography, economics, sociology etc. all over the world. Inter-regional mobility is inter-related with a number of geographical, socio-economic and political factors. As in so many other dimensions of human behaviour, there are apparently no laws of migration. Migration is never certain, it is more or less probable. Numerous attempts are being made to study this interesting phenomenon of spatial mobility and its related factors by both descriptive and mathematical methods. Based on certain observed regularities, general behaviour, cause-effect relationship, some of the attempts proceed towards building scientific models and generalization of migration and interaction. It appears in all the studies that certain observable regularities in movement pattern may be related to spatial variations in amenities and opportunities.

The work done in this book is related to spatial mobility in Rajasthan. It is found, prevailing inter-regional disparities with regard to geophysical, socio-economic and political factors are the push and pull forces for migration. Rajasthan is one of the largest states of India and has large potentialities for future development. After Independence, a little change has occurred in the structure of Rajasthan. But still it is not able to provide job opportunities and other amenities and facilities to its own population. That is why, out-migrants from the state are more than in-migrants. In the study, various models are built to highlight the relative importance of various factors in the process of migratory movement. It is found, developed regions are the centres of attraction for the migrants as the migrant's decision is rational in choosing the place of residence. In this process, resistance offered by distance is higher for rural-ward migration. Moreover, this deterrent effect is less for educated migrants.

Though this study does not make any policy suggestions directly, but it provides the guidelines to the policy-makers in identifying the factors responsible for regional imbalances, which are the causes of migration. Migrants are the direct and indirect costs to both, the sending and receiving, societies. Balanced development of all the regions is the solution of this problem.

My greatest personal debt is to my Guide, Prof B.C. Mehta, Professor, Department of Economics, Sukhadia University, Udaipur, who conceived, detailed and shaped the problem and provided sagacious guidance throughout the present study. His scholarly suggestions, prudent admonitions, immense interest and affectionate behaviour have been a source of great inspiration to me.

I wish to express my intellectual indebtedness to the authors, whose works have been cited in the text of the thesis. I am grateful to Shri P.M. Jat, Assistant Professor in Computer Science, CTAE, Udaipur, for his kind assistance and guidance in my computer work.

I take this opportunity to express my grateful thanks to my former teachers and senior colleagues Mrs K. Padliya, Associate Professor of Economics, Sukhadia University, Dr. G.M.K. Madnani, Associate Professor of Economics, Sukhadia University, Udaipur for their wise advice and assistance during my study.

I shall remain ever grateful to my parents and in-laws for

the constant encouragement and inspiration during the period of this study.

A special word of appreciation is due to my husband, Shri Vinod Kohli, for his kind help and liberal assistance in varying ways in the completion of my study.

Last but not the least, I am grateful to the ICSSR, New Delhi, who have sanctioned the grant to publish this work. I owe a deep sense of gratitude to my publishers, for undertaking the publication of this book.

**Mrs. Anju Kohli**

# *List of Tables*

# 1

# *Introduction*

## 1.1. SPATIAL MOBILITY—AN OVERVIEW

This Chapter is divided into seven sections. In Section 1.1 an overview of spatial mobility is described. Section 1.2 gives the need for the study. Section 1.3 presents objectives of the study. In Section 1.4 scope of the study is discussed. Methodology is given in Section 1.5. The source of data are indicated in Section 1.6 and the design of the study is given in Section 1.7.

Mobility, movement and migration marked the growth and development of all societies. Disparity and imbalances in the growth patterns, the relative deprivation of individuals and groups, dissatisfaction with the social and natural environment among the people, the emergence of new opportunity structures, desire for improved socio-economic status and concern for preservation of liberty, freedom, marriage and disasters—both physical and social—figured among the causes for mobility, movement and migration of individuals and groups spatially and socially (Bogue; 1952).

Mobility may refer to the opportunity, willingness and the factor of change from one place to another and from one level to another. Movement refers to the general process of change among individuals or groups. However, migration refers to the spatial movement of people in pursuit of the fulfilment of certain specified goals for certain period of time or on a permanent basis (Lakshmanna; 1989). These specified goals may be related with push factors at the original place of residence or to the pull factors operating at the intended place of residence resulting in the spatial movement of the people.

Migration often has been declared to be one of the three major subjects that comprise the field of formal demography. The other two subjects are mortality and fertility. These three phenomena are known as the components of population change, for they are the mechanisms by which a population grows or declines in size. A community or nation can gain population only through the fertility of its inhabitants or by migration and it can lose population only through deaths among its residents or by migration. As a component of population change, migration occupies a central place in demographic analysis. It is the major unknown component of population estimates and forecasts. "Potential migrants do not have either perfect or complete information. Their decisions are not deterministic, but inherently statistical, migration is never certain, only more or less probable". (Fogarty & Mehta, 1984). Migration has been variously analysed as a long-term human capital investment, as a selective response of more energetic and adaptable individuals to the changing distribution of economic activity and as the summation of presumably assymmetric push and pull factors associated with the individual and his environment (Todaro, 1969).

Migration frequently is a major symptom of basic social change. Every region and every nation that has undergone extensive industrial development has simultaneously undergone a redistribution of its population. The migration process has a profound effect both upon the areas to which migrants have flowed and upon the areas from which they have come.

Migration is a necessary element of normal population adjustment and equilibrium. Within most nations, some areas have higher birth rates than others. Also some areas are of expanding opportunities for employment while other areas are of stationary or declining economic opportunities. By siphoning off excess population into areas of greater opportunity, internal migration becomes a mechanism of personal adjustment for the citizen and for a nation.

Migration is an arrangement for making maximum use of persons with special qualifications. The special abilities of a particular person are useful to the nation only at certain sites and persons who possess or acquire special abilities are not necessarily born or educated at the site where their talents are needed. Migration moves these specialized persons to the communities where their services can be used efficiently.

Migration is an instrument of cultural diffusion and social integration. The person who migrates from one community to another units in himself in two cultures. Temporarily, he tends to be a disruptive force in the community, into which he enters only by a slow process of assimilation, which sometimes requires a generation or more, the migrant group and the receiving country are finally adjusted to each other. In this process, the culture of the receiving community may be altered appreciably, where internal migration distributes representatives from each region throughout all other regions, the resulting cultural diffusion can contribute to a reduction of inter-sectional and inter-regional differences and to a building up of a common nation-wide culture within which regional variations persist but perhaps are less deviant from each other than otherwise they might be (Bogue; 1952).

The study of inter-regional mobility assumes special importance in the process of development. By its very nature, migration is related to a process of change occurring within the social system. Relationship between migration and economic development can also be seen in terms of the selectivity of the people. In the opinion of Kuznets, migrants are dynamic, risk bearing persons, who respond favourably to economic stimuli and have capacity to detach themselves from traditional surroundings and adapt themselves to unfamiliar environment. They may thus be among the most productive from the stand point of economic growth (Kuznets; 1966).

## 1.2. NEED FOR THE STUDY

Migratory movements are product of the social, cultural, economic, political or physical circumstances in which individuals and societies find themselves (Mehta; 1975, 1978). It is thus a response of human organism to economic, social and demographic forces in the economy. Economists are interested in the study of migration because it is related to business cycles, supply of skilled and unskilled workers, growth of industries and occupations and employment status of migrants. Planners and policy-makers are concerned with migration because it is associated with the socio-economic development of the country. The Indian Planning Commission recommended as early as in 1956 that studies should be undertaken on problems related to regional development with special reference to urbanization. Apart from studying the spatial characteristics of population, an analysis of migration helps solving some of the basic regional problems. Direct population projections must be supplemented by in and out-migration estimates in order to be useful in systematic planning for the development of a region. Geographical mobility is interrelated with a number of socio-economic, political and psychological factors. Moreover, as in so many other dimensions of human behaviour, there are apparently no laws of migration (Mitra, 1967).

Rapid population growth in the less developed regions of the world, substantial increases in the size of urban population and in the levels of urbanization and a sharp rise in the number and size of big cities, all argue for increased attention to population movement as a key component in population dynamics and in urban and rural development (Premi, 1983).

It seems, the relationship between migration and

development is not usually seen in this light in developing countries, particularly in India. The main human problem of migration in the low income countries is that people are mostly moving from unemployment to under-employment from one kind of poverty to another, resulting in a colossal waste of human resources and great human misery. Unlike in developed economies, where migration occurs in association with a qualitative change and vertical shift in the labour force, migration in the low income countries occurs as a spatial system of disease of underdevelopment and regional disarticulation in the space economy (Bose, 1965).

Recent writings on the subject give the impression that the modern industrial sectors of urban centres in developing countries have grown at a very small pace. As a result, migrants attracted initially by the high wage in the modern or organized sectors have had to take up work in the informal traditional unorganized or the murky sector. It is generally argued that the income or wage in the urban traditional sector is not very much different from that in the rural sector, yet it is observed that migration to the urban area has continued in increasing numbers. The contribution of such migrants to the urban economy is considered to be marginal or negligible as most of them are engaged in socially unproductive occupation. The problem is even greater if the migrants were in more productive occupation before migration. The urban economy, however, incurs direct and indirect costs as a result of immigration. Housing, sewage and water facilities, schools, transport and other amenities have to be provided for incoming migrants. The problem thus becomes more acute if the larger urban centres attract a "lion share" to the city and migrants grow at a faster rate than the total urban population in the country. This precisely is the situation in India.

The migrants create a moral problem in the community at which he arrives. It can lead to inter-growing tensions and unrest. Experience had been that second generation and third generation descendants of migrants are well accommodated to the community to which their parents or grand parents moved (Bogue; 1952).

Thus, spatial movements have changed the demographic, economic and social structure of many countries or regions. They have both positive and negative effects on the economy. They have contributed to rapid urbanization on a global scale with its attendant problems acute in countries but encountered also in varying degrees even in developed countries, of congestion, shortage of housing, pressures on the physical and social infrastructure environmental pollution and social tensions and conflicts in the cities. At the same time, the migrants have made a major contribution to economic development in the countries or regions. In the immediate post war period, they contribute to reconstruction of war-raged economies. They relieved shortage of skilled or unskilled labour or a critically needed professionals and took up arduous, unpleasant jobs which the nationals of the countries were reluctant to. From the mid-1970s, however, with the growing unemployment in host countries, particularly of western Europe, the presence of large number of migrants has led to tensions and occasional conflicts between them and nationals. The governments of the host countries under increasing pressures from their nationals have taken legislative and other measures to restrict migrants and to encourage the migrants to return to their home countries.

## 1.3. OBJECTIVES OF THE STUDY

1. To compute and understand the lifetime and decadal intra-district, inter-district and inter-state (1971, 1981) in, out and net migration (rural-urban, rural-rural, urban-rural and urban-urban) in districts of Rajasthan.
2. To prepare inter-district population flow matrices (1971, 1981).
3. To develop reasonable hypotheses to examine the

theories of migration and to test the hypothesis with Rajasthan.

4. To develop models for explaining migratory movements in districts of Rajasthan and to implement test models.
5. To suggest appropriate policies.

## 1.4. SCOPE OF THE STUDY

The present study is conducted at two levels and at two points of time, 1971 and 1981.

(a) at state (Rajasthan) level.

(b) at district level.

The study is confined to 26 districts of Rajasthan. The major concern is to discuss the process of migration in 26 districts and during 1961-71 and 1971-81. The factors affecting the migration process are divided into two—pull and push factors. Migration is a response of human organism to economic, social and demographic forces in the environment (Mehta, 1978). The factors which are likely to counter the process of migration as well as the factors which need to be encouraged in order to make migration meaningful and purposeful are highlighted.

Inter-regional variations in migration have been dealt with at two points of time with the help of contingency tables. Hypotheses regarding the relationship between the dependent variable, migration and the different geographical, economic and social explanatory variables have been constructed on the basis of past literature and theory. Different statistical linear regression models have been built up. They are estimated, tested and interpreted with the help of step by step regression OLS.

The study is based on the secondary and cross-section data. In such studies the problem of multicollinearity is generally encountered principal component analysis is applied to devise orthogonal indicators. The method takes care of intercorrelated variables (Amitabh Kundu; 1980). To remove the effect of heteroscedesticity, weighted regression should be applied (Johnston; 1985, Mehta & Mehta; 1987). However, as the weights are not much different, Arun C. Mehta (1990) tried both the methods of weighted and unweighted regression in his work on population growth in Rajasthan and found no significant difference in his results, so in the study simple unweighted regresssion have been performed.

The study deals with the only one-way relationship i.e. the impact of geo-physical, social and economic variables on migration. But there may be two-way causation for some of the explanatory variables i.e. migration may also influence them. This is excluded from the study, which may cause the problem of simultaneity bias in the results. This problem may be solved by building the simultaneous equations models. The fear of simultaneity bias is reduced by taking the lagged explanatory variables. Moreover, in the absence of multicollinearity, OLS procedure generally gives good results (Johnston; 1985), Mehta & Mehta (1991) have developed the regional demographic-economic interaction model and found that the system turns out to be recursive. In recursive models, OLS applied to each equation produce unbiased and consistent estimates.

The relative importance of the variables is revealed by (a) the coefficients of the variables; (b) elasticities of the co-efficients and (c) the (t) ratio on the co-efficients. To test the structural change-over time, Chow test is generally used (Maddla, Mehta & Mehta; 1987; 148). It can also be tested by pooling the data in different time periods and introducing a dummy variable for time (Mehta & Mehta, 1987; 159), which has been tried in this study. Due to the severe limitations of the data, many crucial variables could not be included and their proxy variables, for which the information was available, represent them.

In spite of the inadequacies, much significance can be attached to the study for providing information about the specific dynamics of migration which might help planners and public authorities to formulate and implement development plans in removing regional imbalances, which is a characteristic feature of Indian Union.

## 1.5. METHODOLOGY

Migratory movements are product of the social, cultural, economic, political or physical circumstances in which individuals and societies find themselves. Hence, the explanatory variables responsible for the process of migration are mainly economic.

The main tool of the analysis is "Regression-analysis" which centres around five issues:

(a) Specification of the model;
(b) Functional form of the relationship;
(c) Estimation of the regression co-efficients;
(d) Interpretation of the results; and lastly
(e) Model evaluation.

Economic theory performs the task of specification of the model i.e. task of identifying the variables. It also provides us the functional form of the relationship between a dependent and independent variables.

The entire analysis in the present study is dependent on single equation framework by using the ordinary least squares (OLS) method under the classical assumption of—

(a) $E(U_i) = 0$

(b) $E(U_i^2) = \sigma_U^2$

(c) $E(U_i U_j) = 0; \; i \neq j$

It is assumed linear relationship exists between a variable

Y and K–1 explanatory variables $X_2$, $X_3$, .............. $X_k$ and a disturbance term U. If the sample is of n observations on Y and X's, then the equation can be written as—

$$Yi = \beta_1 + \beta_2 X_{2i} + \beta_3 X_{3i} + \ldots\ldots \beta_k X_{ki} + U_i$$

$$(i = 1, \ldots\ldots\ldots\ldots, n)$$

The β coefficients are to be estimated (Johnston; 1985).

The major problems of OLS estimation are auto correlation; multicollinearity and hetroscedasticity when the OLS does not yield desirable estimates. Auto correlation is a problem of time-series data, which is not likely to arise in this study as this study relates to cross-section data.

Multicollinearity is a situation, in which two or more independent explanatory variables are so highly correlated with one another that it becomes very difficult to disentangle their separate effects on the dependent variable (Mehta; 1987, 201). Problem of multicollinearity may arise for various reasons. Firstly, it is due to an inherent characteristic of many economic variables to move together over times. Secondly, it arises due to use of lagged values of certain explanatory variables in the regression model (Johnston; Madnani; 1988, 262).

A common indication of multicollinearity is a very high $R^2$ and most of (t) ratios are small (less than unity). It is possible to find high $R^2$ and highly significant 't' values for individual coefficients, even though the multicollinearity is serious. This can arise if individual coefficients happen to be numerically well in excess of the true value, so that the effect still shows up in spite of the inflated standard error (Jhonston; 1985). There are also various tests for the presence of multicollinearity (Johnston; Mehta; 1987, 207).

(a) Zero-order correlation coefficient between the two explanatory variables.

(b) In case of more than two explanatory variables, multicollinearity effect may be used.

(c) Step by step regresssion may be used.

(d) The Farrar Glauber test may also give us an indication of multicollinearity (Johnston).

There are also many methods to tackle the severity of the multicollinearity.

(a) The easiest and commonly used method is to drop the collinear variable(s) from the main regression and to re-estimate the equation.

(b) Joint use of both time series and cross-section data.

(c) Increase the size of the sample.

(d) Step by step regression.

(e) Factor analysis.

In the present study, from the above five methods to deal with the problem of multicollinearity, factor analysis and step by step regression methods are applied.

*Factor analysis:* Factor analysis is by far the most often used multivariate technique of research studies. It is a technique applicable when there is systematic inter-dependency among a set of observed or manifest variables and the researcher is interested in finding out something more fundamental or latent which creates this commonality. It seeks to resolve a large set of variables in terms of relative few categories known as factors.

There are several methods of factor analysis, among them the important are—

(a) the centroid method;

(b) the principal components method;

(c) the maximum likelihood method.

In the study, composite indices have been developed

with the help of principal component analysis. This analysis essentially involves an orthogonal transformation of a set of variables ($X_1$, $X_2$, ...............Xp) in a new set of variables ($Y_1$, $Y_2$...............Yp). This transformation results in ($Y_1$, $Y_2$,...................Yp) being uncorrelated with one another, notwithstanding the fact that the original variables ($X_1$,$X_2$,..............Xp) may have been quite highly inter-correlated. There are as many components derived as there are variables and the original total variance associated with ($X_1$, $X_2$,.............Xp) is preserved exactly in the total variance of the components ($Y_1$, $Y_2$,................Yp). The solution of the principal component analysis was outlined originally by Hotelling (1933). The assumption that we are dealing with multivariate normal distribution is not essential for the principal component solution unless certain inferential questions are posed. If the original variables are standardized i.e. with zero means and unit variances, then the variance-covariance matrix becomes the matrix of simple correlations (R). Moreover, in this case the total variance equals P, the number of variables. The eigen values in turn will sum to P (King; 1969).

The procedure for the principal component analysis is firstly to find out the latent or characteristic roots from the following :

$$| R - \lambda I | = 0$$

Where $\lambda$'s are the latent roots. Corresponding to the first root or eigen value of this equation is a column vector or eigen vector ($a_{11}$, $a_{21}$, ..................... $ap_1$), which when normalized by the factor ($a^2 11 + a^2\ 21 +$ .............. $a^2\ p_1$) yields the coefficients ($W_{11}$, $W_{21}$, ..................., $Wp_1$) i.e.

$$(R - \lambda I)\ a_1 = 0$$

such that $a_1', a_1 = 1$

Then compute the weighted average of the standardised

variants by using the elements of (W) as weights. Thus the first principal component is—

$$Y_1 = W_{11}X_1 + W_{12}X_2 + \dots\dots\dots W_1pXp$$
$$Y_i = W_{i1}X_1 + W_{i2}X_2 + \dots\dots\dots W_ipXp$$

and so on.

The coefficients in the matrix [W] are in fact the correlations between the original variables and the components. These coefficients are often referred to as the loadings of the variables on the components. The component loadings are not invariant under a change of the measurement scales for the variables. The mathematical consequences of such changes are discussed in Anderson (1958). The principal component analysis is most useful when the variates $X_i$ are measured in the same units. The uses of ranked data or standardized variates are partial answers to this problem.

The interpretation of the principal components in research problem is done mainly with reference to the loadings (weights), the variants having high correlation or loadings on a component will serve to identify that component. On any component some variables will have low loadings and consequently will be ignored in the process of giving an interpretation to the component. On these particular variables some observations will certainly have high values in the original data matrix and their scores on the component will be weighted accordingly by the unimportant variables.

The question of how many components should be interpreted is a vexing one. Bartlett (1958) has derived test for the hypothesis that the (P–K) eigen values remaining after the 'k' largest one have been extracted are equal. Lawley (1956) and Masewell (1962) point out that these tests are not exact in the case when standardized variables are being analysed. A convenient rule of thumb seems to be to evaluate all components with eigen values equal to or greater than one, or alternatively, to evaluate each one which accounts for a sufficiently high proportion, say at least 5% of the total variance.

Principal component analysis and its variants are held in high esteem by regional scientists, because of their optimality properties. In regional analysis often one has to identify and evaluate varying regional configuration of activities or other characteristics and factors of growth and also their inter-relationships. One feels safe in recommending this method as it also takes care of multicollinearity (Dasgupta; 1971, Kundu; 1980).

Another method adopted to deal with the problem of multicollinearity is *step by step regression*. This method involves adding one independent variable at a time and generating a series of intermediate regression equations. The first independent variable considered is the one which has the highest simple correlation with the dependent variable. This initial two variable regression is completed and then the partial correlations between the dependent and all the other independent variables are computed. The independent variable among these which has the highest partial correlation, in other words the one which contributes most to the unexplained variation in the dependent variable, remaining after the first regression is then included in the second step. A new regression equation now involving two independent variables is derived; the partial correlations are computed for the remaining variables with the two held constant and the selection of the next variable to be included is made on the basis of these values. At each step, the adjusted partial regression co-efficient and multiple correlation also are computed. The step-wise procedure continues until all the specified independent variables are included (King; 1969).

Thus, we estimate number of regression equations and the one which gives the highest $R^2$ is selected. Stepwise regression analysis is an extension of multiple regression analysis.

Multicollinearity is though a serious problem, one should not concern with whether or not multicollinearity exists but to what extent it exists. Multicollinearity is not necessarily a problem, unless it is highly relative to the overall degree of multiple correlation among all variables simultaneously. That is (Klein; 1969, 102) collinearity is not harmful if $r^2 x_i, x_j < R^2 y, X_1, X_2, \ldots\ldots, X_n$ where $r^2 x_i x_j$ is the simple correlation between two explanatory variables ($X_i$ and $X_j$) and $R^2$ is the overall (multiple) correlation of the relationship.

In many econometric studies, especially those based on cross section data, the assumption of a constant variance for the disturbance term (assumption of homoscedasticity) is unrealistic Johnston (1985). This problem of heteroscedasticity, though provides unbiased OLS estimates, but the variance of the OLS coefficients are large and also the OLS estimates are inefficient, (Johnston; 1985). To remove the effect of heteroscedasticity, weighted regression must be performed (Mehta & Mehta; 1987). A.C. Mehta (1990) tried both the methods but found no significant difference in the results. Therefore, simple unweighted regression has been performed.

The problem of simultaneity bias due to reverse causation may also arise which necessitates the building of simultaneous equation model. This problem is reduced by taking the lagged explanatory variables. Moreover, Mehta & Mehta (1991) have developed the regional Demographic Economic Interaction Model and found that since the system turns out to be recursive, OLS provides biased estimate.

The 't' ratio to test the significance of the estimated co-efficients is obtained by

$$t = \frac{\beta^n - \beta}{S.E\,(\beta^n)}$$

Generally, the variables having the 't' value less than unity are dropped and regression is re-run on the remaining variable or an alternative is to apply step by step regression, which has been applied in the study with the critical value of F = 1 for the inclusion or exclusion of a variable.

To test the stability or relationship or whether there has been a structural change over time, Chow test is generally used (Maddla; 1989, 268) i.e. to test $H_0 : B_{11} = B_{21}, B_{12}, = B_{22}$ .............. B1k = B2k,.......$a_1 = a_2$ for the B's the first subscript denotes the data set and the second subscript denotes the variable. An alternative is to pool the data for the different periods under consideration,pooling increases the efficiency of the estimates (Hannan and Young; 1977).

## 1.6. SOURCES OF DATA

The study is based on the secondary data. The sources of data are the publications of Directorate of Economics & Statistics (Raj.), Government of India, and Government of Rajasthan. The publications are the following:

Source of Data on Population and Migration

1. Census of India 1971, Series-18, Rajasthan, Part II-A General Population Tables.
2. Census of India, 1971, Series - 18, Rajasthan, Part II--D, Migration Tables.
3. Census of India 1981, Series-18, Rajasthan, Part II-A, General Population Tables.
4. Census of India, 1981, Series-18, Rajasthan, Part II-D, Migration Tables.
5. Census of India, 1981, Series-18, Rajasthan, Part II-B, Primary Census Abstract.
6. Census of India, 1981, Series-1, India, General Population Tables.

7. Census of India, 1971, Series-1, India, General Population Tables.
8. Census of India, Migration Tables, 1981, D-Series, Part V.

**Source of District-wise Data on Geo-physical and Socio-economic Indices**

1. Statistical Abstracts, Rajasthan, 1972, 1977 and 1980.
2. Basic Statistics of Rajasthan 1972, 1982.
3. District Census Handbooks (1971, 1972, 1973, 1982, 1983).
4. Agricultural Statistics and Plan Progress (1971-72, 1972-73, 1981-82 and 1982-83).
5. Report on Agricultural Census (1970-71, 1971-72, 1980-81 and 1981-82).
6. Report on Annual Survey of Industries, Rajasthan (1970-71, 1980-81), Directorate of Economics and Statistics.
7. CMIE, Basic Statistics relating to Indian Economy, Vol. 2, States.
8. A Technical Note on the Seventh Plan of India (1985-90).
9. Rajasthan Budget Study (1989-90).
10. Some facts about Rajasthan, 1987 (DES; 1989).

The data of the study are given in Table A-1.1 and A-1.2 (Appendix) in the end.

## 1.7 . THE DESIGN OF THE STUDY

The study is divided into nine Chapters. The first Chapter gives an overview of spatial mobility, need for the study, objectives, methodology and scope of the study. The second Chapter is survey of literature of varying aspects of migration. The third Chapter discusses Rajasthan's geophysical and economic setting and the factors explaining regional variation in migration. In the fourth Chapter, pattern of migration is analysed. In the fifth chapter inter-district migration linkages are developed, migration clusters are identified and they are correlated with development clusters. In the sixth Chapter, district in-migration models are built. Seventh Chapter deals with inter-district migration models. The eighth, Chapter concludes all the Chapters and points out the limitations of the study and policy implications to the policy-makers.

# 2

# *A Brief Review of Relevant Works*

Mobility, movement and migration marked the development of societies. Migration is purely a socio-economic phenomenon, which is a result of a complex mechanism involving social, psychological, economic, political institutions and other determinants. It is a selective procedure in which individuals with certain socio-economic characteristics and different sets of opportunities are more likely to migrate than others.

This chapter presents in brief review of some important works. Numerous attempts have been made and are being made to study this interesting phenomenon of spatial mobility and its related factors by both descriptive and mathematical methods. Studies made by the researchers are of a wide variety covering different aspects of spatial mobility. Some studies analyse prevailing migration trends, some throw light on the factors influencing migratory movements. Some are related with inmigration whereas others are concerned with outmigration. There are four types of migration streams, rural to rural, rural to urban, urban to rural and urban to urban. Many studies are concerned with different types of migration streams. Some studies are general while others are specific relating to a particular continent, country state or region.

The present chapter highlights these studies and the factors which are considered for the migration models in the subsequent chapters.

The major task of migration research, therefore, is—

(a) to identify the nature of these socio-economic characteristics;

(b) to devise appropriate measures of both characteristics and opportunities;

(c) to specify appropriate relationship between personal characteristics, alternative economic opportunities and propensities to migrate on the basis of well formulated and plausible theoretical models;

(d) to estimate relative quantitative significance of different factors influencing either the propensity of individuals to migrate or the aggregate rate of migration;

(e) to devise quantitative productive estimates of the impact of alternative policy approaches designed to influence cne or more of the independent variables identified as significant factor affecting the decision to migrate in a particular country or a region (Salvatore, 1970).

Any technical study of migration constitutes one or more of the following areas of research:—

(a) Estimation of migration from direct or indirect data, including rate of migration.

(b) Migration differentials and trends.

(c) Determinants of migration process;

(d) Demographic, social, psychological, economic and other implications of migration (Misra, 1981).

V. Nath (1986) described that most of the studies on migration are addressed to the question—who migrate why they do it, what satisfaction or relief from their original homes do they seek in migration? How they decide where to go,what problems do they face as a result of migration, how, by whom and why are the migrants provided with the information required to take the decision to migrate and choose the place of migration and work there? Is migration by individual or by groups, is it permanent, long-term, temporary, short-term, seasonal or year throughout? What problems do the migrants create in the places of migration? What adjustments are required by the older residents of these places to solve or mitigate these problems? What new perceptions, attitudes the migrants and the order residents must take so that the two groups can live in peace and harmony without conflicts or tensions.

K.C. Zachariah (1980), considered problems relating to measurement of internal migration and projections of sub-national populations. He described methods for measuring in-out and net migration using census data:

1. Direct period-specific question on migration;
2. Survival ratio method using age-distributions for two years;
3. Place of birth survival method;
4. Combined estimates of migration and mortality rates. He noted difficulty of predicting future migration trends and said best predictor of future trends is past trends.

## 2.1. MIGRATION TRENDS

*Migration trends* have been analysed in various studies. D.M. Bohra (1969) analysed various aspects of internal migration in Rajasthan e.g. migration behaviour of the population, types of migration, regional pattern of migration and rural-urban migration in detail.

S.C. Srivastava (1971) presented an analysis of migration in India using data from the 1971 census. Both qualitative and quantitative aspects of migrants are assessed and the factors influencing migration are considered. S. Mukerji (1979) used 1951, 1961 and 1971 Indian census data to study migration trends. The study revealed rural-urban migration decreased in 1951-61 compared to 1941-51 period. Comparison of 1961-71 estimate showed a continuing slackening in urban-urban migration. Urban-rural or back migration increased at this time. The two explanations for this phenomena are (1) that rapid population growth in the cities without concomittant economic development and greater number of jobs resulted in the "push back" movement or (2) that the economic improvement in the agricultural sector lured once rural-urban migrants back to rural areas. It is estimated future population growth in urban areas will result from natural increase rather than from rural-urban migration.

K.S. Murty and K.R. Murty (1980) analysed the pattern of internal migration in the State of Maharashtra using 1971 census data for the period 1961-71. The nature, volume and directions of migration are examined. Migrants are characterised according to factors including age, sex, marital status, occupation and areas of origin and destination.

M.K. Premi (1983) analysed the intercensal migration and classified the migrants into four categories, rural-rural, rural-urban, urban-rural and urban-urban. And the migration distance is (a) Intra-district (b) Inter-district (c) Inter-state.

B.C. Mehta (1978) analysed salient features of internal migration in India and in Rajasthan. He concluded that migration in India is much smaller than in the western countries, bulk of migrants are females, rural-rural migration is a predominant feature of migration. Rural to urban migration is small proportion of total migration, major proportion of migration is short distance. The principal purpose of migration is demographic. Remigration and repeat migration as well as very short duration migration are quite frequent, the sex ratio decreases with the distances moved.

## 2.2. FACTORS INFLUENCING THE MIGRATORY MOVEMENTS

There are studies which emphasized the various factors *influencing the migratory movement*. Greenwood (1969, 1970), Veddls & Gallaway (1972), Devy & Wallycki (1973) among others attempted to account for family-friend effect by including a migrant stock variable in their explanatory variables.

The analysis of B.N. Sarkar (1980) showed that the social problems among the less educated or illiterate backward communities represented by scheduled caste Hindus and Muslims in Bengal were significant push factors from ancestral homes. Whereas the economic consideration shaped the migration of other educated social groups.

Goldstein (1976) in his study emphasized that rapid population growth in the less developed regions of the world, substantial increases in the size of urban population and in the levels of urbanization and size of big cities all argue for increased attention to population movement as a key component in population dynamics and in the urban and rural development. The need to monitor such movements has been accentuated by the continued substantial increase in the rural population which in many countries place ever growing pressures on the limited resources available to support such growing numbers and contributes to extensive rural to rural movements as well as shifts from rural to urban places.

A study by V.N.P. Sinha (1980) analysed various approaches taken by different scholars towards definite typology and decision-making perspective connected with the phenomenon of migration. Factors responsible for different types of migration have been analysed in detail. The second half deals with life cycle and socialization of migrant's career pattern, urbanization and impact of migration on donor and receiving society.

P. Schultz (1982) in his study analysed migration as a long-term human capital investment, as a selective response to more energetic and adaptable individuals to the changing distribution of economic activity and as the summation of presumably asymmetric push and pull factors associated with the individual and his environment. All of these approaches posit an individual moving to where his future appears most attractive, or more formally to where he maximizes the present (discounted) value of future streams of benefits minus costs (opportunity, direct and psychic), subject to his limited knowledge of the world and his preferences.

Migrants can be classified into four migration streams (a) Rural to rural (b) Rural to urban (c) Urban to urban (d) Urban to rural.

## 2.3. RURAL-URBAN MIGRATION

In many studies, one of these streams has been analysed. *Rural to urban migration* is regarded as a necessary concomitant of industrialization and modernization. M.P. Todaro (1967) in his study highlighted,rural to urban migration is stimulated primarily by rational economic cosiderations of relative benefits and costs, mostly financial but also psychological. The decision to migrate depends on expected rather than actual urban rural real wage differential where the expected differential is determined by the interaction of the two variables, the actual urban rural wage differential and the probability of obtaining employment in the urban modern sector. The probability of obtaining an urban job is inversely related to the urban employment rate. Migration rates in excess of urban job opportunities growth rates are not only possible but also rationale or probable in the face of continued positive urban rural expected income differentials.

Ashok Mitra (1967) in his study speculated that rural to urban migration will decline in volume and velocity, because of a high degree of urban to urban migration in India, as well as rapid natural increase of urban population, it would be more difficult for the rural population to find jobs in urban areas.

Anjana Desai (1978) discussed the monetary impact of rural urban migration on the migrants specially on the labour force. The concept of relative earnings and how it differs from absolute earnings has been discussed. I. Adelman and S. Robinson (1978) found rural urban migration pattern to influence subsequent distribution of income within the society. Migration tends to raise the agricultural terms of trade and rural incomes, it also lowers the rural-urban income differential.

A.S. Oberoi and H.K. Manmohan Singh (1981) emphasized in their study that migration is beneficial to the individual migrants and will continue until the underlying basic factors causing wide rural urban and inter-urban differential in wages and employment opportunities are altered.

Shekhar Mukherji (1981) noted the problems of unemployment and under-employment and under-employment resulting from extensive rural-urban movements in developing countries. A mobility field theory model is developed, at the level of both the individual and the aggregate system to provide a theoretical basis for understanding the complex of factors that lead people to move as well as to generate clues for migration mobility.

Rural-urban migration is often times a response to income differences and uneven distribution of economic opportunities between regions, migration is justified as an equilibrium factor which reduces regional income differential over time by redistributing labour in proportion to available job opportunities. But the empirical research undertaken in the LDCs highlighted the ills or explosive consequences of unabated rural-urban migration in these countries (ILO 1965, 1969, 1972 studies).

Sudha Deshpande (1983) in her study highlighted these consequences particularly in relation to urban unemployment and rapid growth of a low productive informal sector and the social ills to the deterioration in the quality of urban life arising from inadequate growth of the urban infrastructure in relation to the demand for it.

## 2.4. RURAL-RURAL MIGRATION

*Rural to rural migration* is an important phenomenon. It is growing in magnitude with the development especially in developing countries. C.H. Shah and B.V. Patel (1979) attempted in their study to explore the forces affecting these movement and their impact on economic well-being of communities from which people move in for work. It is found in the study rural-rural migration benefits both the receiving and the supply regions. However, the benefits of migration seem to be unequally distributed. In receiving region unequal distribution is in terms of likely increase in inequality of inter-income class income distribution. In labour supplying region, inequality is linked to increase spatially, the small and distant villages not benefitting or benefitting less than the large and well connected villages.

M.K. Premi (1983) noted rural-rural migration has declined but it would remain a dominant stream in Indian migration for several decades, particularly till the end of the present century.

D.K. Kothari (1983) explored the role of household structure and size in order to understand the issues involved in rural-rural migration. The study revealed that migrants tend to come from large households and to be younger siblings. The study concludes it may be a deliberate strategy for a large household to diversify the portfolio of human capital in order to increase or maintain its economic position in the village, or to reduce dependence on risky income and output from the family's economic activity. This explanation views the household as the maximizing welfare unit and migration as a way of achieving a more productive distribution of labour.

## 2.5. URBAN-URBAN AND URBAN-RURAL MIGRATION

*Urban-urban and urban-rural migration* has increased according to 1971 census in comparison to 1961 census (Premi) from the social mobility point of view and considerations of economic development, this may prove to be a healthy trend.

M.K. Premi (1980) examined the nature, causes and consequences of urban-urban migration in India. Chapters are included on demographic and social-economic differentials between towns experiencing out-migration and those experiencing in-migration, characteristics of out-migrants and patterns of out-migration, characteristics of in-migrants and consequences of out-migration.

## 2.6 OUT-MIGRATION

M.K. Premi (1976) analysed some of the *characteristics of out-migrants* and studied the pattern of their out-migration. Some of the major findings of the analysis are the predominance of females in out-migration due to the system of exogamy in marriage, the major out-migrants belong to the age group of 15-34, possesses higher educational qualifications than their counterparts at home and out-migrants have significantly higher earnings than the resident workers. It has been concluded that it is not the absolute level of push and pull forces, but the differentials in them which govern the volume of migration.

## 2.7 MIGRATION POLICIES

Some studies are centered round the policies which govern the migratory movements. M.P. Todaro (1978) examined the determinants and consequences of internal migration in the context of policy choices available to governments in developing industries. Various migration-influencing and migration-responsive policies are examined and evaluated. He concluded most governments in developing countries are more concerned with problems of population distribution than population growth. Specifically, problem of rapid urbanization resulting from unprecedented rural-urban movements of people have risen in recent years to the top of the development policy agenda.

Although continued rural-urban migration is inevitable and in most situations desirable part of the development process, the tendency of the governments to focus their development efforts on a small modern industrial sector often to the neglect of rural development has created severe economic and social imbalances in income-earning opportunities between urban and rural areas. As a result, migratory flows in many less developed countries have been greatly in excess of urban job creation, giving rise to the phenomenon of urban unemployment and urban marginalism.

Goldsteins, S. (1979) made efforts to assess the relationship between population movement and the problems of cities and rural areas, as well as the formulation of policies and programmes designed to deal with these problems. S.E. Findley (1979) examined rural development programmes that have been implemented to increase rural productivity and incomes and to decelerate rural migration rates. He discussed explicit programme objectives, details of programme design and expected outcomes in way of employment, income and migration as well as types of migrants and development strategies that have increased migration rates.

A.B. Simmons (1979) studied the restrictions, regulations, control, disincentives and other socio-economic measures that slow and reverse the rural-urban migration. He concluded, the decision to slow urban growth in developing countries relies on the cost of population.

## 2.8. MIGRATION MODELS

Based on certain observed regularities, general behaviour, cause-effect relationship, some of the attempts proceed towards building scientific models and generalization of migration and inter-regional population interaction. Evidence from simple analysis of survey data allows to observe the relationship of only two variables at a time—that is the relationship between migration and one other explanatory variable. Thus it is not possible to weigh the relative importance of the variables, except what can be seen is whether correlation is weak or strong. The validity of such a method also requires the assumption that the explanatory variables are orthogonal to each other, this may, however, not be true.

Three distinct conceptual approaches underlie the literature on migration models. These may be defined as the size-distance theories, the push-pull theories and probabilistic theories of migration. The size-distance theories tend to be formulated as gravity models, push-pull theories as regression models and probabilistic theories as stochastic processes and simulation models.

English demographer, E.G. Ravenstein (1889) made first formal use of the Newtonian model in a social science context, who contended after analysing the migration data that a population centre attracted migrants from other centres in direct proportion of both the sending centre and the receiving centre raised to some power. The potential concept of the *gravity model* may be thought of as a measure indicating the intensity of the possibility of interaction. Young (1924) contended that movement varies inversely with the square of distance between source and terminal areas. Reilly (1929) proposed a law of retail gravitation which states that a city attracts retail trade from a customer to its size and inverse proportion to the square of the distance separating the customer from the centre of the city. The major impetus in the development of the gravity model comes out from the work of Zipf (1946) and Stewart (1948).

According to Carrothers (1956), the gravity concept of human interaction postulates that an attracting force of human interaction between two areas of human activity is governed by the population masses of two areas and a friction against interaction is caused by the intervening space over which the interaction must take place.

P.A. Klown (1971), having tested the validity of a population migration model proposed by Ravenstein (1889), worked out an alternative construct which incorporated and supplemented the step-wise process to obtain a better picture of movement patterns.

Sahariah (1983) used the potential concept of the gravity model to calculate the probability of an individual moving from one district to the other in a bid to estimate the urban-ward as well as rural-ward inter-district migration in Assam based on 1961 census data.

Many statistical *regression models* have been built to emphasize the pull and push forces influencing migration. Mildred, B.L. and Wadycki, W.J. (1974) formulated a regression model to test the effect of foregone opportunities on the allocation of inter-state migration in Venezuela. C.H. Shah and B.V. Patel (1979) used the step-wise regression model to study rural-rural migration. The hypothesis tested in the model is that out-migration will respond better to pull factors, which is supported by the results. Jonathan, K. (1978) established a utility maximisation framework for the migration decision. The basic idea is that an individual chooses to live in the area which gives him the maximum present value of the discounted net earning stream. A statistical regression model is built to test the implications of the theory.

B.C. Mehta (1975, 1978) in his multivariate regression

model combining the gravity and push-pull models has concluded that migrants from short distances outnumber those from long distances as far as out-migration from Rajasthan is considered. But in the case of in-migration to Rajasthan, though mainly migrants come from the adjoining states, yet the states having the longest border with the state do not send the largest number.

G.S. Fields (1979), F. Thomas and D. Mehta (1984), J.J. Brennan (1987) used the *logit model* to study the effects of various factors on migration. Porter (1973), Jones (1974), Elek (1976), Andrew (1983) by using the *simulation techniques* examined the migration in detail.

The study of A.D. David (1982) is concerned with the application of different types of models to the study of migration flows.

## 2.9. SOME ECONOMETRIC MODELS SUMMARISED

Econometric migration research tends to take two objectives but closely related forms, micro and macro. They are reflected in the choice of dependent and independent variables. The micro-economic approach for estimating migration asks the basic question, what is the probability or propensity an individual will migrate from source i to destination area j. In macro studies, the dependent variable is gross rate of migration expressed as the proportion of population Pi, that migrates to destination j over a specified period of time. Moreover, the micro migration is based on survey data and macro on census data. However, some of the explanatory variables in both the studies may be common. A brief view of some of migration econometric models are given in Table 2.1.

Most of the econometric migration studies, whether micro or macro, use O.L.S. techniques especially with logarithmic specification for estimating the parameters.

**TABLE 2.1**

**Summary of the Different Models**

| S.No. | *Name of the author* | *Specification* | *Estimation* | *Independent Variables* |
|---|---|---|---|---|
| 1 | 2 | 3 | 4 | 5 |
| 1. | M.J.Hay (1980) | (a) $P_i = P(U_i R_i c_i r_i n_i z_i)$<br>>0 <0 <0 <0 >0 | Probit analysis functions $U_i$ and $R_i$ are estimated by O.L.S. in semi-log form. | $U_i$, $R_i$ expected income in urban and rural areas,<br>$r_i$ - rate of interest to discount.<br>$n_i$ - length of planning.<br>$z_i$ - the error term. Horizontal<br>$AGE_i$-age at the time of migration. |
| | | (b) $P_i = a_0+a_1U_i+a_2R_i+a_3AGE_i+Z_i$ | | |
| 2. | T. Paul Shultz (1982) | Logistic or log linear model<br>(a) $P_{ij} = \frac{e^{zij}}{\sum_{j=1}^{n} eij}$ | Maximum likelihood technique<br>O.L.S. can be applied | Characteristics of origin and destination area. |

*(contd.)*

| 1 | 2 | 3 | 4 | 5 |
|---|---|---|---|---|
| | | $Z_{ij} = (+ \Sigma LNX_{ki} + \sum_{k=1}^{n} rLNx_{kj} + SLND_{ij}$<br>(b) Double log equation to estimate migration and its determinants.<br>$LNM_{ij} = \beta_{ij} + \beta_1 LN\ N_i + \beta_2 LNN_j + \beta_3 LND_{ij} + \sum_{k=4}^{n}\beta\ KNx_{k\text{-}3i} + \Sigma\beta_t LNX_{L-nj}$ | | |
| 3. | G.S. Fields (1977) | Log - Linear<br>(a) $M_{ij} = f(E_i, E_j, C_{ij}, E', C_{ij}')$<br>(b) Straight line specification<br>$Mij = \alpha + \beta_1 E_i + \beta_2 E_j + \beta_3 C_{ij4} \overline{\beta}_4$ Demog.+u | Maximum Likelihood Estimation | Zone's income and employment opportunities, cost of alternative possibility, Cost of migration, demographic variables |
| 4. | M.T. Carvazal and D.T. Geithman (1974) | $\frac{Mij}{Pij} = bo_i + b_{ijk} Y_{ijk} + b_{2i} U_{ij} + b_{3i} E_{ij} + b_{4i} D_j + b_5 S_{ij} + U_i$ | Least Square Method | The level of local wages and salaries, the level of local average education, estimate |

*(contd.)*

| 1 | 2 | 3 | 4 | 5 |
|---|---|---|---|---|
| | | | | average distance from farm to nearest large town and extent of coverage under social security system. |
| 5. | B. Sahariah<br>A. Borthakur<br>(1984) | Gravity Model<br>$l_{ij} = \int \left( \frac{M_{id}}{D_{ij}} \right)$<br>$l_{ij} = aM_1^{b1} M_2^{b2} d_{ij}^{-b3}$<br>$Pij = \frac{WjTij^{-\alpha}}{\sum_{j=1}^{n} Wj\ Tij^{-\alpha}}$ | O.L.S. Method | The distance between i & j and some measure of the mass of the interacting pair of places. |
| 6. | Annable (1972) | Simultaneous Equation Model | Reduced form and two-stage Least Squares | Real wage rate of U-R. |

*(contd.)*

| 1 | 2 | 3 | 4 | 5 |
|---|---|---|---|---|
| 7. | H.Y. Parh and H.H. Fullerton (1980) | Simultaneous Equation Model (nine sets of equations) | Two-stage Least Squares | U-R labour force, natural increase of population level, level of employment and unemployment. |
| 8. | D. Salvatore (1970) | Simultaneous Equation Model (Three first order difference) | Full Information Maximum Likelihood Method | Difference in average unemploy-rate, average wage per employed worker, natural % growth in labour force, difference in the % of labour force employed in agriculture, % of growth in real value added in industry. |
| 9. | Jonathan King (1978) | Utility Maximisation Framework $U_k = U_k (x_1, x_2, x_3, ......x_p)$ | O.L.S. | Discounted present value of the expected real wage stream, the expected rate of return to physical capital, |

*(contd.)*

| 1 | 2 | 3 | 4 | 5 |
|---|---|---|---|---|
| | | $mix = G(u_i \ u_k)$<br>$mix = M_o k (x_{ij}, x_{ijk}, \ldots\ldots, x_{pi}, x_{pk})$<br>$\frac{SM_{ij}}{n_1} = \frac{m_{ij}}{n_i} = M_{ij} (\overline{x}_{ij}, \overline{x}_{1i}, \overline{x}_{pi}, \overline{x}_{pj})$ | | the direct and opportunity cost of moving, the psychic costs and benefits. various psychic costs and benefits. |
| 10. | M.P. Todaro (1969) | Based on expected R-U income differential | | Discounted present value of the expected urban real income stream discounted present value of the expected rural real income stream, natural rate of increase of the labour force, probability of selecting from the pond of urban traditional workers, total modern sector employment, rate of job creation, rate of |

*(contd.)*

| 1 | 2 | 3 | 4 | 5 |
|---|---|---|---|---|
| | | | | industrialisation, rate of labour productivity growth in the modern sector. |
| 11. | B.C. Mehta (1978) | Linear<br>(a) State Level<br>$M_i = a_o + a_1p_i + a_2s_i + a_3d_i + a_4cb_i + a_5y_i + a_6pd_i + a_7Edi + a_8v_ia_9\ y_{agr} + a_{10}gp + a_{11}p_{0i} + a_{12}l_i + v_i$<br>(b) District Level<br>$M_i = a_o + a_1p_i + a_2p_i + a_3y_i + a_4u_i + a_5w_i + a_6sc_i + a_7pp_i + u_i$ | Multivariate Regression Analysis | Distance, standard of living, water resources, proportion of SC/ST, Population of the district population potential. |
| 12. | M.B. Levy and W.J. Wadycke | Double Log | Conditional Probability | Distance, Population, Unemployment rates, monthly |

*(contd.)*

| 1 | 2 | 3 | 4 | 5 |
|---|---|---|---|---|
| | (1974) | (a) $A_{ij}\begin{pmatrix} d_{ij}p_jU_j, w_j, \\ p^*, u^*, w^* \end{pmatrix}$<br>(b) $A_{ij} = \frac{M_{ij}}{\sum_{j=1}^{n} M_{ij}}$ | is calculated | wages. |
| 13. | A.P. Bartel (1979) | Linear Probability Equations<br>$PM_t = f(G_t)$<br>$G_t = Y_t^* - Y_t - C_t$ | Maximum Likelihood Logit Estimates | Individual characteristics, family characteristics and job related characteristics (discounted net gain from moving). |
| 14. | James A. Dunlevy and Henry A. Gemery (1977) | Koyck-type log model | O.L.S. | Migrant Stock, Population, Per capita income, Temperature and Distance. |

## 2.10. FACTOR INFLUENCING MIGRATORY MOVEMENTS

In the study following factors are considered in migration models. Hypotheses are developed and tested in subsequent chapters.

1. *Density of population:*
   Person living per sq km of area.
2. *Capital Towns:*
   Number of capital towns in each district.
3. *Per capita plan expenditure:*
   It is measured in rupees.
4. *Distance* in kilometre of the district headquarters from the nearest two cities.
5. *Degree of urbanization:*

$$\frac{\text{Total urban population of the ith district}}{\text{Total population of the jth district}} \times 100$$

6. *% of literates* to total population.
7. *% of literates* with some schooling.
8. *Total number of educational institutions* in a district.
9. *Density of roads* per 10,000 sq km of area.
10. *Density of railways* per 10,000 sq km of area.
11. *% of registered factories* to total number of factories in Rajasthan, i.e.

$$\frac{\text{Total number of registered factories in the ith district}}{\text{Total number of factories in Rajasthan}} \times 100$$

12. *% of workers in manufacturing industries* to total workers.
13. *Per capita value added in manufacturing industries*

$$\frac{\text{Total value added in manufacturing industries in Rs. in the ith district}}{\text{Total population of the jth district}}$$

14. *Per capita capital employed in manufacturing industries*

$$\frac{\text{Total capital employed in manufacturing industries in Rs. in the ith district}}{\text{Total population of the jth district}}$$

15. *Pumps + Oil Engines:* Number of pumps + oil engines per 1000 hectares of gross irrigated area.

$$\frac{\text{Total number of pumps + oil engines}}{\text{Gross irrigated area}} \times 1000$$

16. *Tractors:* Number of tractors per 1000 hectare of net sown area:

$$\frac{\text{Total number of tractors}}{\text{Net sown area}} \times 1000$$

17. *Power consumption in agriculture per hectare of gross cropped area in kilowatts.*

$$\frac{\text{Total power consumption in agriculture}}{\text{Total cropped area}}$$

18. *Livestock per hectare of net sown area i.e.*

$$\frac{\text{Total number of livestock}}{\text{Net sown area}}$$

19. *Agricultural Labourer* = % of agriculture labour to total workers for each district.

20. *Consumption of fertilizers per 10 hectare of gross cropped area in kilograms.*

$$\frac{\text{Total consumption of fertilizers}}{\text{Gross cropped area}} \times 10$$

21. *% share of wells and tubewells.*
22. *Normal rainfall in centimeters*
23. *Irrigation extent*

$$\frac{\text{Gross irrigated area}}{\text{Gross cropped area}} \times 100$$

24. *Irrigation intensity*

$$\frac{\text{Gross cropped area}}{\text{Net sown area}} \times 100$$

25. *Land productivity equals*

$$\frac{\text{Agricultural output}}{\text{Gross croped area}}$$

26. Agricultural output is expressed in rupees. It is obtained by taking first five principal crops according to the sown area. Then the output of each crop relating to each district is multiplied by corresponding average harvest prices. The sum total is agricultural output.
27. *Labour productivity in agriculture equals*

$$\frac{\text{Agricultural output}}{\text{Number of agricultural labourers + cultivators}}$$

28. *Commercialisation of Agriculture*

$$\frac{\text{Total area under cash crops}}{\text{Gross cropped area}} \times 100$$

In commercial crops, all major cash crops considered in statistical abstract are taken.

29. *Per capita availability of foodgrains* (per day in grams)

$$\frac{\text{Total availability of foodgrains}}{\text{Total population} \times 365}$$

30. *Scheduled Caste and Scheduled Tribes % of SC/ST* is measured to the total population.
31. *Total number of commercial banks* in each district.
32. *Cooperative credit:* Loans advanced by cooperative societies per hectare of gross cropped area in terms of rupees.
33. *Doctors* per lakh of population.
34. *Hospital beds* per lakh population.
35. *Migrant stock:* is measured as the number of migrants located in district (who migrated from place) in the period before the census period of 10 years i.e. people living in the district above 10 years divided by the population of the district.
36. *Average age* is defined as the weighted average of people in various 5 years age groups, using the median of each group weighted by the number of people in the group and summed over all groups and divided by total population for each district. The oldest group is open intervaled and we have arbitrarily chosen the median is to be 60 years.

Thus, there is no dearth of literature on spatial mobility. But very few studies are concerned with regional patterns within a state. An attempt has been made in the present work to study the problem at the intra-state level and fill the gap.

# 3

# *Geo-physical and Socio-economic Salient Features of Rajasthan*

This Chapter is focused on the geo-physical and economic setting of Rajasthan and the factors influencing migratory movements in the state. The Chapter is divided into four sections.

Section 3.1 presents geo-physical features. Section 2 deals with socio-economic features and Section 3 shows at a glance the regional differences in socio-economic features. Section 4 gives the conclusion.

## 3.1 GEO-PHYSICAL FEATURES

Rajasthan is a land of diversity. It is India in miniature in so far as its diverse geographic, cultural and economic character is concerned. Prior to independence of the country in 1947, the State of Rajasthan did not exist as a political entity, though as cultural entity Rajasthan had been in existence for centuries. The present State of Rajasthan was formed after Independence as a result of the merger of erstwhile princely states and the former part of States of Ajmer as well as transfer of small enclaves from one state to another, which commenced on March 17, 1948 and ended on November, 1956. Prior to integration, Rajasthan was a conglomeration of ninety princely states and three chiefships varying in size, population, revenue, political importance and awakening, administrative set-up and state of socio-economic development.

The State of Rajasthan is characterized with distinct geographic features. It is situated in north western part of India, lies between 23° 3' N and 30° 12' N latitudes and 69° 30' E and 78° 17' E longitudes. It is surrounded in north and west by Pakistan, in north-east by Punjab and UP, south east by MP and south-west by Gujarat. It covers the geographical area of 342,239 sq kms (1981 census) divided into 27 districts. In area, it is the second largest state of India, first being MP. Rajasthan's share in all India figures comes to 10.74% in area, 4.76% in population and it contributes only 3.1% of north India (NSS Report; 1988).

**Topography**

The topography of Rajasthan is dominated by the Aravali system of mountains running south to north through the heart of state. The area lying to the west of Aravali slopes towards Indus Valley and towards the Rann of Kutch. This area possesses undulating topography and is covered by sand-dunes showing general ridges parallel to the wing direction. The only river of importance in this area is river Luni which originates from the Nag Hills near Ajmer. The Ghaggar having its course in north of Bikaner brings some water during the rains. The region characterised by the eastern side of Aravali is a diversified region. The river Chambal and its tributaries — Banas, Kali, Sindh, Parwati add to the importance of the eastern plateau. The river Mahi flowing through Dungarpur and Banswara in the extreme south and Banganga traversing through Jaipur and Bharatpur and the Knan, Kothari, Mansi, Gambhiiri, winding through Bhilwara, Udaipur, Banswara and Dungarpur districts also contribute for the diversified topography of the region.

**Physiography**

The Aravali system of hills dominate the physiographic features of the state. Based on the existing physiographic features, the state can be divided into seven distinct divisions—

1. Aravali hills system;
2. Eastern Plains;
3. South Eastern Plains;
4. Southern Plains;
5. Alluvial Plains of the mid-west;
6. Sandy Plain and Desert Pedo Plain;
7. North West Flood Plain.

The "Thar" district occupies a dominant position in its physiography. The western and north western part of the Aravalis are full of sand and the most western part is called the "thar" desert.

**Climate**

Though the state in general is to face extreme climatic conditions, the weather conditions are clearly demarcated by the Aravali hill range. The area lying west of Aravali is characterized by great extremes of temperatures and long period of severe drought accompanied by high wind and low humidity. The eastern side of Aravali is a complex region with considerable variation in rainfall as well as range of temperature. The state on the whole has 3 distinct seasons with varied durations. (1) Hot weather (2) Rainy season (3) Cold weather. According to Rajasthan Ground Water Board (1983-84), the climatic features divide the State into four main regions — (a) Arid (b) Semi-arid (c) Sub-humid (d) Humid. Table 3.1 shows 11 districts comprise the arid zone, 7 semi-arid zone, 4 sub-humid zone and 4 humid zone.

With the number of rainy days less than 20 days per year, the western part of Rajasthan is chronologically drought affected area. It has been subject to famines from the earliest times. One lean year in three and one famine year in eight, is the usual expectation (Budget Study, 1987-88). One of the main causes of the lean or famine year is the unreliability of rainfall.

**TABLE 3.1**

**Regions of the State According to Water Resources**

| | *A. Arid Zone* | *B. Semi-Arid Zone* | *C. Sub-Humid Zone* | *D. Humid Zone* |
|---|---|---|---|---|
| 1. | Barmer | Ajmer | Bundi | Banswara |
| 2. | Bikaner | Alwar | Chittorgarh | Dungarpur |
| 3. | Churu | Bharatpur | Sirohi | Jhalawar |
| 4. | Sri Ganga Nagar | Bhilwara | Udaipur | Kota |
| 5. | Jaisalmer | Jaipur | | |
| 6. | Jalore | Swai Madhopur | | |
| 7. | Jhunjhunu | Tonk | | |
| 8. | Jodhpur | | | |
| 9. | Nagour | | | |
| 10. | Pali | | | |
| 11. | Sikar | | | |

Source: Rajasthan Ground Water Board (1983-84).

### Rainfall

The rainfall is uneven, erratic and scanty and varies widely in the state. The dominant geological feature in Rajasthan, the Aravali range almost completely arrests the already faltering summer monsoon, creating a semi-arid and desert zone of the west and a more watered region in the east. The unreliability of rainfall has subjected Rajasthan to frequent famines. There are great inter district differentials in rainfall as well as variability of rainfall (Mehta, 1978).

### Mineral Resources

Rajasthan has a large variety of mineral resources which have begun to be properly mined and organized only after independence of the country and integration of the princely states.

Over 30 important minerals, both metallic and industrial and a large variety of building stones are found and worked in the state. In the desert region the Eocene formation yields lignite coal. In the north western regions are found limestones, porous sand-stones and the region is believed to be potentially rich in oil. Fuler's warth, bentonite and gypsum are some of the other minerals in the region. The central Aravali area produces mica, beryl, felspar, quartz, tenntalite etc. There are several good limestone quarries, red stone and marble quarries also. Rajasthan has large potentiality in metallic mineral deposits. Copper is already being extracted while zinc smelting has also begun. Minerals important to iron and steel industry such as tungsten and manganese are also found in the state. Salt is another mineral found in Rajasthan. Thus, the state has large geo-physical variation.

## 3.2 SOCIAL AND ECONOMIC DEVELOPMENT

Neither the western nor the eastern portion of the state is a homogeneous area, but as a rule, the parts of the state that reach towards the Gangetic plains and the Deccan are conducive to rainfed agriculture and have higher population densities. Irrigation facilities, road and rail services and modern industry are more common in parts of the east, but they are very unevenly distributed even there and are not unknown in the west. The large canal works of the upper Ganges Valley reach fingers into the far north-west corner of Rajasthan's desert making Ganganagar district outstandingly suitable for agriculture. Elsewhere in the dry west, the sheer lack of agricultural opportunity has favoured dependence on household and other industry, and population is often bunched in towns located where geographical conditions are comparatively advantageous.

The economy of Rajasthan has a unique position in the country. It has shown sharp fluctuation in its performance in its plan periods due to various natural and geographical factors. In the past, Rajasthan was regarded as a backward region in the backward economy of India.

The economy of Rajasthan is predominantly agrarian. Its

total rural working population was about 87 lakh in 1981, out of which about 71.9 lakh i.e. 82.6% were engaged in agriculture and other allied activities like forestry, livestock etc. The percentage of urban population in Rajasthan in 1981 was 21.04 as compared to 23.31 for all over India (Census of Rajasthan, 1981).

The most glaring feature of the State's economy has been its highly unstable nature. The State was in the grip of famines during the four years from 1984-85 to 1987-88, so much so that all its 27 districts had to be declared famine affected during the last two years. The instability in the state economy particularly in the agricultural sector is visible in annual fluctuation in crop output. It is estimated that the output of foodgrains in 1987-88 was 48 lakh tonnes, which is likely to reach a record level of 105 lakh tonnes due to good monsoon. Similarly, during this period the output of cotton is likely to increase from 2.5 lakh to 5.5 lakh tonnes. These instances indicate the highly volatile and unstable nature of the state economy and point towards its unsteady and uncertain behaviour. The net state domestic product of Rajasthan increased from about Rs 1654 crores in 1970-71 to about Rs 2383 crores in 1987-88 at 1970-71 prices. Thus it has witnessed sharp fluctuation from year to year. (Rajasthan Budget Study 1989-90).

There is little modern industry and per capita income lags behind the Indian norm. The annual growth in industrial production during 1971-85 has been of the order of about 6% (DES, 1969) Per capita income has declined between 1970-71 to 1982-83 from Rs 620/- to Rs 579/- whereas in India the same has increased from the level of Rs 633/- to Rs 712/-. The rate of growth was only 0.3% per year during the period 1960-80. (Draft Seventh Five Year Plan (1985-90);(Mehta; 1985). Thus the gap between Rajasthan and India as a whole has widened. In fact, this relative deterioration has been the sharpest in the case of Rajasthan among the seven northern region states.

The population of the state increased by 33% during 1971-78, which was substantially higher than the national average of 25%. It is likely to reach the level of 5 crore by 1996 (Ashok Bapna, 1989). The percentage growth rate of population in the decades 1951-61 and 1961-71 was 26.20 and 27.83 respectively in Rajasthan as compared to 22.51 and 24.80 in the same period for India. (Some Facts About Rajasthan, 1987 (DES, 1969). Thus, it is seen that the growth of population in Rajasthan is always higher than that of all over India. This is a retarding factor for the growth of the state. On average, Rajasthan is by Indian standards sparsely populated. Though it constitutes a little more than 10% of the total area of the country, only 5% of the country's population resides in the state. The population density is the lowest for any major state. Varying definitions of poverty line have given various estimates of proportion of people living below poverty line, but the levels of consumption indicated by NSS data reveal that almost 50% of the state's population is below poverty line, which proves its relative backwardness. The Technical Note on the Seventh Plan of India (1985-90) shows that the poverty-ratio in Rajasthan increased from 33.6% in 1977-80 to 34.3% in 1983-84 while the all India average in this respect came down from 48.3% to 37.4%.

The development indices of the key indicators for India as well as for Rajasthan and the rank of Rajasthan among all the states is given in Table 3.2

The information given in the Table (3.2) gives us a glimpse of Rajasthan's economy and its worse economic position in Indian economy as compared to other developed states and national averages. Rajasthan's rank in all the development indicators is lower among the states covered. Literacy rate indicator shows 22nd position of the state among the 22 states covered. This rank is linked with the rank of per capita plan expenditure on education, in which the state is having 21st position among the 25 states covered. Similarly other indicators

**TABLE 3.2**

**Rajasthan—in Indian Economy**

| *S.No.* | *Item* | *Unit* | *Per Year* | *All India* | *Rajasthan* | *States covered* | *Rajasthan's rank among states covered* |
|---|---|---|---|---|---|---|---|
| 1 | 2 | 3 | 4 | 5 | 6 | 7 | 8 |
| 1. | Per capita income at current prices. | Rs. | 1986-87 | 2974 | 2150 | 24 | 18th |
| 2. | Index of development of infrastructure. | Rs. | 1987-88 | 100 | 78 | 24 | 17th |
| 3. | Literacy rate. | % | 1981 | 36 | 24 | 22 | 22nd |
| 4. | Per capita rural income from agriculture. | Rs. | Average of 1984-85 to 1986-87 | 32.8 | 43.4 | 23 | 8th |
| 5. | Consumption of fertilizers per hectare of gross cropped area. | Kg. | 1987-88 | 51.2 | 12.4 | 25 | 20th |

*(contd.)*

| 1 | 2 | 3 | 4 | 5 | 6 | 7 | 8 |
|---|---|---|---|---|---|---|---|
| 6. | Per capita value added in factory sector. | Rs. | 1985-86 | 307 | 162 | 21 | 14th |
| 7. | Per capita financial assistance distributed by All India financial. institutions | Rs. | 1987-88 | 83 | 63 | 25 | 13th |
| 8. | Per capita advances by scheduled commercial banks. | Rs. | 1988 | 1108 | 556 | 25 | 15th |
| 9. | Per capita expenditure on education. | Rs. | 1987-88 | 136 | 132 | 25 | 21st |
| 10. | Hospitals and Dispensaries per 100 sq.km. | No. | 1988 | 11.4 | 4.3 | 25 | 17th |
| 11. | % of rural population covered by potable water supply. | % | 1985 | 56.2 | 58.7 | 25 | 15th |

(contd.)

| 1 | 2 | 3 | 4 | 5 | 6 | 7 | 8 |
|---|---|---|---|---|---|---|---|
| 12. | % of villages electrified. | % | 1989 | 78 | 70 | 25 | 16th |
| 13. | Per capita consumption of electricity. | KW | 1985-86 | 178 | 140 | 25 | 9th |
| 14. | Road length per 1000 sq.km. | Km. | 1982-83 | 473 | 222 | 25 | 21st |
| 15. | Railways per 1000 sq.km. | Km. | 1987-88 | 18.85 | 16.4 | 20 | 13th |
| 16. | Per capita Plan outlay. | Rs. | 1985-90 | 1026 | 718 | 22 | 20th |

Source: CMIE, "Basic Statistics Relating to the Indian Economy" Vol. 2, States, Sept. 1989.

point out Rajasthan's lower rank in comparison to other states. It is a backward state in a backward economy.

In almost all aspects, Rajasthan is lagging behind the very modest Indian economy.

## 3.3 REGIONAL DIFFERENCES IN SOCIO-ECONOMIC FEATURES

Even though Rajasthan is an under-developed state, all its districts are not at the same level of under-development. Table 3.3 shows at a glance regional disparity. Indices and composite indices of different socio-economic indicators have been computed. Their arithmetic mean, standard deviation and coefficient of variation are given in the Table 3.3.

The standard deviation and coefficient of variation indicate the regional heterogeneity prevailing in socio-economic variables. Industrial development index shows the highest variation (99.82%) and the least variation is shown by the water resource index (41.42%) (Mehta; 1978; 15-19). Clustered 26 districts of Rajasthan into homogeneous groups on the basis of various indicators of socio-economic development on the basis of this study (Mehta; 1978), Jaisalmer, Barmer and Jalore are the lowest developed districts followed by a cluster of two districts, Dungarpur and Banswara and another cluster of Jhunjhunu, Sikar, Nagaur and Churu. A cluster of four districts, Alwar, Kota, Bharatpur and Pali is of relatively medium developed districts. And the most developed districts i.e. Sri Ganganagar, Jodhpur, Bikaner, Ajmer and Jaipur form single district cluster independent of each other. Mehta has pointed out that development is isolated but under development is in clusters.

Sharma (1975) developed separate composite indicators of sectoral development using principal component method for the year 1961 and 1971. Mehta (1983) used his indicators of agricultural and economic development to classify the

**TABLE 3.3**

**Indices Level and Variability of Socio-economic Development in 26 Districts of Rajasthan 1981**

| | *Density of population per sq km of area Index* | *% of SC/ST to total population* | *Degree of urbanisation* | *Transport Index* | *Industrial Development Index* | *Medical facilities Index* | *Water Resource* | *Mechanisation Index in Agri.* | *Agricultural output Index* | *Banking and Credit Index* |
|---|---|---|---|---|---|---|---|---|---|---|
| Arithmetic Mean | 127.0769 | 25.1915 | 22.7492 | 23.6219 | 1.8619 | 44.9965 | 1.9857 | 1.5615 | 1.9498 | 0.9385 |
| Standard Deviation | 59.1060 | 16.1929 | 13.7174 | 13.3410 | 1.8587 | 31.4167 | .8225 | 1.2989 | 0.9048 | 0.7529 |
| Coefficient of Variation | 46.51 % | 64.27 % | 60.30 % | 56.48 % | 99.82 % | 69.82 % | 41.42 % | 83.18 % | 46.40 % | 80.22 % |

Source: Computed in Chapter VI for model building.

districts into three categories (i) low developed (ii) medium developed (iii) high developed. The low developed districts are those whose level of development is below 15% of the average, high developed are those whose level of development is above 15% of the average and the medium developed districts fall between these limits.

The developed regions do not have wide-spread diffusion effects, so they are not the centre for transmitting fundamental changes in the state's economy.

Thus Rajasthan has a historical lag in economic development. Historically, Rajasthan had the worst kind of feudalistic, economic, political, social and cultural structure, when Rajasthan was formed. There was practically no administration and infrastructure that development was perhaps at the lowest level in India. Political stability, responsive administration and entrepreneurship of its people has led to faster economic development over the last four decades, though it still continues to be relatively less developed State of India. To get rid of this backwardness, planning in Rajasthan should be x-rayed (Mehta; 1985). There should be Planning Board at the state and the district level to plan on the pattern of Planning Commission.

## 3.4 CONCLUSIONS

This Chapter explains the large variation in geo-physical and socio-economic structure of Rajasthan. Different regions of the state are on the different level of development. The plain regions are the developed, the dry regions less developed and the hilly regions are the least developed regions of the state. The economy of the state is predominantly agrarian. In spite of the potentialities and resources, Rajasthan is lagging behind the national stream. The development indices of key indicators point out Rajasthan is having lower rank in comparison to other states. The state has many favourable conditions for economic development. Its people are hard working and adventurous as is evidenced by the entrepreneurial activities of Rajasthani people outside Rajasthan. Rajasthan has got vast resources of minerals and unlimited wealth. Therefore, there is a challenge and an opportunity for the development of the state. For this, overhauling of planning in Rajasthan is required. In fact, what is needed is to plan in a planned way.

# 4

# *Pattern of Migration in Rajasthan—1971, 1981*

Migration is normally defined as a permanent or semi-permanent change of residence entailing a substantial change in social and economic ties to a particular community (Bogue, 1959; Lee, 1966; United Nations, 1970). "It is a process of redistribution of population which is generated due to defective organization of space economy i.e. the socio-economic, disparity steming out of man's relation with geographical diversity, exerts pressures on population to move at least horizontally if not vertically" (Rathore & Premi, 1988).

The concept of migration would be quite simply applied to empirical analysis, if all migrants made single, uni-directional, long distance moves. Migration patterns, however, are often quite complex involving various degrees of permanence and dissolution of community ties (Scott Radloff, 1981). The study of migration data not only indicates the impact of migration on the growth of population, it also reveals the intensity of mobility and the direction of movement of population.

In the Indian census, from 1872 onwards till 1961, migration data were presented with reference to the place of birth. If a person was born at a place other than the place of enumeration, he/she was treated as a migrant in census returns (Rajasthan, Migration Tables; 1961). And a person was non-migrant who had migrated elsewhere for all purposes and happened to be at the place of birth during the period of enumeration. In 1961 census, an effort was made to widen the scope of enquiry. Information was collected on (i) Birth place (ii) Birth place (R, U) (iii) Duration of residence, if born elsewhere. These statistics did not account for the more recent movement of a person.

In 1971 census, migration data were collected for the first time on the basis of place of last residence, in addition to the question for birth of place. The questions were—

*I. Birth Place:*

(a) Place of birth;
(b) Rural/Urban;
(c) District; and
(d) State/Country

*II. Last Residence:*

(a) Place of last residence;
(b) Rural/Urban
(c) District;
(d) Duration of residence at the village or town of enumeration.

In 1981 census, the scope of enquiry on migration has been further widened by collecting information on reasons for migration from place of last residence in addition to the enquiry made in 1971.

One of the basic characteristics of the population obtained through the census is its rural/urban distribution. The basic unit for rural areas is the revenue village which has definite surveyed boundaries. In unsurveyed villages within the forest areas each habitated area, with locally recognised boundaries has been treated as one unit.

Urban areas have been specially defined for census purposes. In the 1981 census, the same criteria as accepted in

1961 and 1971 census have been adopted with some minor variations. Urban areas in 1981 census consist of—

(a) All places with a Municipal Corporation or Cantonment Board or Notified Town Area.

(b) All places which satisfy the following criteria—

  (i) A minimum population of 5,000.

  (ii) At least 75% of the male working population being engaged in non-agricultural (and allied) activities.

  (iii) A density of population of at least 400 per sq km (or 1,000 per sq. miles).

The urban criteria of 1981 vary slightly from that of 1961 and 1971 census, in that the male working in activities such as fishing, logging etc. were treated as engaged in non-agricultural activities and therefore contributed to the 75% criterion in 1961 and 1971 census, whereas in 1981 these activities have been treated as on par with cultivation and agricultural labour for the purpose of this criterion.

Based on place of birth (or last residence) and place of enumeration, migrants can be classified into four migration streams (a) rural to rural (b) urban to urban (c) rural to urban (d) urban to rural.

Migrants can further be classified according to distance:

(a) Intra-district migrants: Persons enumerated within the district of birth (or last residence) but not in that particular place.

(b) Inter-district migrants: Persons born (or with last residence) outside the district of enumeration but within the same State.

---

1. Census of India, 1971, 1981 Series-18, Rajasthan, Part-A General Population Tables.

(c) Inter-state migrants: Persons born (or with last residence) in a State/Union Territory of India other than that of enumeration.

(d) International migrants: Persons born (or with last residence) in a country other than enumeration.

The study is focused on short distance (Intra-district), medium distance (inter-district) and long distance (inter-state) migration of Rajasthan with the combination of four migration streams—rural to rural, rural to urban, urban to rural and urban to urban.

This Chapter is divided into two Sections—Migration at State level and Migration at District level. In Section 4.1, analysis of migratory movement in 1971 and 1981 is given as a whole. In Section 4.2 analysis of migratory trends of districts for the same two periods are given.

Spatial unit state/district is taken to mean in terms of the census nomenclature. Their boundaries are changeable from census to census.

Table 4.1 shows at glance in 1971 census, 29.76 per cent of the total population is enumerated out of the place of birth, whereas in 1981 census the percentage of in-migrants is 29.80. The population of the state has also gone up due to natural increase of the population and a little bit due to in-migration.

Table 4.1 points out distance is a substantial deterrent to migration. Migrants tend to move to cities and towns in their own state or region, but they will move longer distances if the destination, wages and job opportunities are considerably higher. "Distance is a traditional proxy for migration costs—psychic, pecuniary and opportunity" (Schultz; 1976). Table 4.1 shows at a glance negative effect of distance on migration. The percentage of intra-district (short distance), inter-district (medium distance) and inter-state (long distance) in-migrants for the 1971 census is respectively 19.17, 5.85 and 3.34 and for

**TABLE 4.1**

**Percentage Distribution of Lifetime in-Migrants in Rajasthan by Place of Birth (1971, 1981)**

| S.No. | *Place of birth* | *Person* | | *Percentage of population* | |
|---|---|---|---|---|---|
| | | *1971* | *1981* | *1971* | *1981* |
| 1. | Born in the place of enumeration | 18,098,078 | 24,054,473 | 70.24 | 70.20 |
| 2. | Born elsewhere in the district of enumeration (short distance migration) | 4,939,934 | 6,341,202 | 19.17 | 18.60 |
| 3. | Born in other districts of India (medium distance migration) | 1,509,597 | 2,394,673 | 5.85 | 6.93 |
| 4. | Born in other states of India (long distance migration) | 855,868 | 1,232,318 | 3.34 | 3.59 |
| 5. | Born in other countries plus unclassified (international migration) | 362,329 | 239,196 | 1.40 | 0.69 |
| | Total population of Rajasthan | 25,765,806 | 34,261,862 | 100.00 | 100.00 |

Source: (a) Census of India 1971, Series-18, Rajasthan, Part II-D Migration Tables (b) Census of India 1981, Series-18, Rajasthan, Part II-D, Migration Tables.

the 1981 census it is 18.60, 6.92 and 3.59. A little decrease in the short distance in-migrants is visible, whereas the percentage of the medium and long distance in-migrants has gone up by little. It may be due to the (a) little change in socio-economic development of the districts, or (b) due to increase in the educated people. "Education interacts with the cost of distance variable. The better educated person have a comparative advantage in longer-distances moves being more adept at adopting and evaluating information on distant job opportunities (Schultz; 1976). In spite of this decrease in short distance in-migration, it dominates the lifetime in-migration stream in 1971 and 1981.

**TABLE 4.2**

**Percentage Distribution of Lifetime In-Migrants for Four Different Migration Streams in 1971,1981 (Place of Birth Data)**

| *S. No.* | *Migration Stream* | *1971* | | | *1981* | | |
|---|---|---|---|---|---|---|---|
| | | *Male* | *Female* | *Sex ratio* | *Male* | *Female* | *Sex ratio* |
| 1. | Rural to rural | 58.37 | 81.31 | 4699 | 52.43 | 77.42 | 5000 |
| 2. | Rural to urban | 20.48 | 7.53 | 1240 | 24.89 | 9.25 | 1258 |
| 3. | Urban to rural | 7.29 | 5.20 | 2408 | 7.07 | 5.91 | 2826 |
| 4. | Urban to urban | 13.86 | 5.96 | 1450 | 15.61 | 7.42 | 1612 |
| Total | | 100.00 | 100.00 | | 100.00 | 100.00 | |

Source: Computed from:

(a) Census of India, 1971, Series-18, Rajasthan Part II-D Migration Tables.

(b) Census of India 1981, Series-18, Rajasthan Part II-D Migration Tables.

Table 4.2 shows rural to rural in-migration stream dominates in both the censuses of 1971 and 1981. The preponderance of female in-migrants is more glaring due to exogamy system of marriage prevailing in Indian society. The strength of this female migration is less in urban areas. The strength of rural to rural stream declined in 1981 in comparison to 1971, more so in the case of males, raising the sex ratio still further. In 1981 it is five times of males. Premi (1983) observed that in 1971 rural to rual migration in India has declined in comparison to 1961, but it would remain a dominant stream in Indian migration for several decades, particularly till the end of this century. This fact is supported by this study of Rajasthan. Rural to urban migration is next to rural to rural migration and is also sizeable. It is more in 1981 in comparison to 1971. Rural to urban migration is mainly economic in nature and accompanies the process of modernization and industrialization. Migration from urban areas i.e. urban to rural and urban to urban indicates a social mobility. Urban to urban has shown a rising trend, this may prove to be a healthy trend whereas the urban to rural is more or less same in both the periods 1971 and 1981. The sex ratio increases in all the four stream in 1981 in comparison to 1971.

Table 4.3 indicates migration in Rajasthan is limited by the boundaries of the districts. The pace of the integration of districts is very slow. Intra-district migration (53.61) dominates the three distance stream. Rural to rural flow decreases with the distance moved. It is clear from the Table 4.3 inter-state rural to rural in-migration is a little higher than inter-district in-migration. It may be due to the large number of bordered districts of the state. Their distance with the other states is less in comparison to other districts of the state. The sex ratio decreases with distance moved. It indicates solo migration of males for economic reasons.

As the migrants are further classified by duration of residence at the place of enumeration, it is easy to get estimates of migrants within last one year (current migrants), inter-censal (decadal migrants) and those who move prior to the last census i.e. stock of migrants (Mehta; 1978). In all these cases, the estimates relate to the survivors of the migrants in each time interval.

TABLE 4.3

**Percentage Distribution of Lifetime In-Migrants in Twelve Types of Migration Stream Based on Place of Birth Data 1971, 1981**

| S. No. | Types of Migration | 1971 | | | 1981 | | |
|---|---|---|---|---|---|---|---|
| | | Male | Female | Sex ratio | Male | Female | Sex ratio |
| 1 | 2 | 3 | 4 | 5 | 6 | 7 | 8 |
| 1. | INTRA-DISTRICT | | | | | | |
| (a) | Rural to rural | 71.22 | 87.26 | 4956 | 64.15 | 84.26 | 5569 |
| (b) | Rural to urban | 18.69 | 6.58 | 1432 | 23.23 | 7.64 | 1695 |
| (c) | Urban to rural | 5.83 | 3.93 | 2731 | 6.23 | 4.73 | 3222 |
| (d) | Urban to urban | 4.36 | 2.23 | 2074 | 6.39 | 3.37 | 2110 |
| | Percentage to total migrants | 53.61 | 67.92 | | 55.37 | 65.83 | |
| II. | INTER-DISTRICT | | | | | | |
| (a) | Rural to rural | 39.58 | 69.52 | 4972 | 38.65 | 65.08 | 4733 |
| (b) | Rural to urban | 25.11 | 9.86 | 1111 | 28.72 | 12.47 | 1095 |
| (c) | Urban to rural | 8.96 | 7.86 | 2463 | 24.92 | 14.63 | 1563 |
| (d) | Urban to urban | 26.35 | 12.82 | 1381 | 7.74 | 7.82 | 2777 |
| | Percentage to total migrants | 26.96 | 22.39 | | 26.57 | 22.58 | |
| III. | INTER-STATE | | | | | | |
| (a) | Rural to rural | 41.14 | 62.97 | 2869 | 38.85 | 58.47 | 2876 |

*(contd.)*

| 1 | 2 | 3 | 4 | 5 | 6 | 7 | 8 |
|---|---|---|---|---|---|---|---|
| (b) | Rural to urban | 21.63 | 10.55 | 923 | 23.65 | 12.14 | 990 |
| (c) | Urban to rural | 9.69 | 8.59 | 1677 | 29.09 | 20.46 | 1373 |
| (d) | Urban to urban | 27.54 | 17.89 | 1215 | 8.39 | 8.93 | 2049 |
| | Percentage to total migrants | 19.43 | 9.69 | | 18.06 | 11.59 | |

Source: Computed from:

(a) Census of India 1971, Series-18, Rajasthan, Part II-D, Migration Tables.

(b) Census of India, ·1981, Series-18, Rajasthan, Part II-D, Migration Tables.

Table 4.4 shows at a glance, the proportion of male migrants among the all duration male migrants for the rural to rural stream in the current period is 5.55 in 1971 and 5.32 in 1981 whereas this proportion for the inter-censal period is 17.85 and 18.73 respectively for the medium and longer distance this proportion has declined further. This also applies to rural to urban, urban to rural and urban to urban stream for the current and intercensal period in 1971 and 1981.

While looking at the sex ratio, decadal migration is female selective, it is higher in the inter-censal period than current period. Current migration is economic in nature whereas inter-censal is mainly demographic and family migration.

Table 4.5 reveals intra-district migration (short distance) for males and females, for the current and inter-censal period, dominates in all duration migration for 1971 and 1981 for the longer distance, the percentage goes on declining due to negative relation of distance and migration.

TABLE 4.4

**Percentage Distribution of Current and Intercensal In-Migrants in Twelve Types of In-Migration Streams Based on Duration of Residence 1971, 1981**

| S.No. | Types of Migration | 1971 CURRENT | | | 1971 DECADAL | | | 1981 CURRENT | | | 1981 DECADAL | | |
|---|---|---|---|---|---|---|---|---|---|---|---|---|---|
| | | Male | Female | Sex ratio | Male | Female | Sex ratio | Male | Female | Sex ratio | Male | Female | Sex ratio |
| 1 | 2 | 3 | 4 | 5 | 6 | 7 | 8 | 9 | 10 | 11 | 12 | 13 | 14 |
| I. INTRA-DISTRICT | | | | | | | | | | | | | |
| (a) | Rural to rural | 5.55 | 3.03 | 1690 | 17.85 | 16.16 | 2796 | 5.32 | 2.34 | 1409 | 18.73 | 16.88 | 2895 |
| (b) | Rural to urban | 1.18 | 0.28 | 750 | 5.53 | 1.62 | 904 | 1.19 | 0.25 | 665 | 6.73 | 2.00 | 958 |
| (c) | Urban to rural | 0.95 | 0.28 | 912 | 2.72 | 1.10 | 1246 | 0.79 | 0.19 | 800 | 3.75 | 0.79 | 678 |
| (d) | Urban to urban | 0.45 | 0.14 | 975 | 1.88 | 0.72 | 1179 | 0.43 | 0.13 | 940 | 2.09 | 0.91 | 1399 |
| II. INTER-DISTRICT | | | | | | | | | | | | | |
| (a) | Rural to rural | 1.91 | 0.95 | 1539 | 4.84 | 4.02 | 2572 | 2.20 | 0.78 | 1138 | 6.12 | 4.49 | 2356 |

| 1 | 2 | 3 | 4 | 5 | 6 | 7 | 8 | 9 | 10 | 11 | 12 | 13 | 14 |
|---|---|---|---|---|---|---|---|---|---|---|---|---|---|
| (b) | Rural to urban | 0.72 | 0.15 | 665 | 2.93 | 0.77 | 810 | 0.66 | 0.15 | 747 | 4.08 | 0.53 | 919 |
| (c) | Urban to rural | 0.70 | 0.19 | 839 | 1.75 | 0.69 | 1219 | 0.58 | 0.13 | 718 | 1.28 | 0.70 | 1754 |
| (d) | Urban to urban | 1.27 | 0.28 | 687 | 1.27 | 0.28 | 687 | 0.73 | 0.22 | 967 | 4.44 | 1.63 | 1180 |
| **III. INTER-STATE** | | | | | | | | | | | | | |
| (a) | Rural to rural | 0.97 | 0.42 | 1450 | 2.93 | 2.11 | 2234 | 0.98 | 0.37 | 1205 | 3.23 | 2.09 | 2076 |
| (b) | Rural to urban | 0.45 | 0.08 | 579 | 1.53 | 0.40 | 817 | 0.31 | 0.08 | 823 | 1.93 | 0.53 | 887 |
| (c) | Urban to rural | 1.16 | 0.16 | 681 | 2.24 | 0.48 | 669 | 0.79 | 0.12 | 482 | 1.58 | 0.46 | 939 |
| (d) | Urban to urban | 0.85 | 0.19 | 681 | 3.34 | 0.99 | 916 | 0.59 | 0.15 | 850 | 3.00 | 1.08 | 1152 |

Source: Computed from:

(a) Census of India 1971, Series-18, Rajasthan, Part II-D, Migration Tables.

(b) Census of India, 1981, Series-18, Rajasthan, Part II-D, Migration Tables.

**TABLE 4.5**

**Percentage Share of Each Stream in Current and Inter-Censal Migration 1971, 1981, Based on Duration of Residence**

| S. No. | *Migration Stream* | *1971* | | | | *1981* | | | |
|---|---|---|---|---|---|---|---|---|---|
| | | *Current* | | *Decadal* | | *Current* | | *Decadal* | |
| | | *Male* | *Female* | *Male* | *Female* | *Male* | *Female* | *Male* | *Female* |
| I | Intra-District | 48.55 | 59.64 | 53.79 | 63.05 | 52.67 | 58.96 | 53.08 | 63.03 |
| II | Inter-District | 27.70 | 25.41 | 27.44 | 25.10 | 28.71 | 26.37 | 28.87 | 24.08 |
| III | Inter-State | 23.75 | 14.95 | 18.77 | 12.85 | 18.62 | 14.67 | 18.05 | 12.89 |

Source: Computed from Census of India 1971, 1981 Series-18, Rajasthan Part II-D Migration Tables.

## INTER-STATE MIGRATION IN RAJASTHAN

Inter-state migration of people may be viewed as a crucial indicator of national integration. The migrant population has to develop an emphatic frame of mind, preparing for exposure to a different cultural milieu, the host state, similarly exhibit a sense of tolerance and accommodation. It is hypothesized that a greater degree of heterogeneity of a population in a provincial state is conducive to national integration. By definition, a heterogenous state is a minor replica of the diversity of a nation's cultural fabric (Gupta; 1984).

At a glance on Table 4.6, it is clear that male out-migrants from Rajasthan are more than the male in-migrants in both the census periods 1971 and 1981. It means that the force of push factors is still more than pull factors. In case of out-migrants, it is the percentage of rural persons higher than urban areas, which shows urban areas of Rajasthan are not able to provide job opportunities to their rural offsprings whereas male migration, in-migration and out-migration, in the state is due to economic reasons, female migration is mainly demographic in the adjoining states, which is clear from the sex ratio. Some female migration may be family migration whereas the wife and other members of the family accompany the earning member of the family.

**TABLE 4.6**

**Percentage of Inter-State In-Migrants and Out-Migrants from Rajasthan Based on the Place of Birth 1971, 1981**

| *Category* | *1971* | | | *1981* | | |
|---|---|---|---|---|---|---|
| | *Male* | *Female* | *Sex Ratio* | *Male* | *Female* | *Sex Ratio* |
| **IN-MIGRANTS FROM RAJASTHAN** | | | | | | |
| TOTAL | 1.37 | 3.34 | 2204 | 2.39 | 4.94 | 1925 |
| RURAL | 1.10 | 3.45 | 2869 | 1.42 | 4.18 | 2730 |
| URBAN | 2.62 | 2.76 | 923 | 5.77 | 7.91 | 1202 |
| **OUT-MIGRANTS FROM RAJASTHAN** | | | | | | |
| TOTAL | 2.59 | 3.37 | 1180 | 3.03 | 4.13 | 1254 |
| RURAL | 2.71 | 2.97 | 1005 | 2.55 | 3.46 | 1260 |
| URBAN | 2.08 | 5.28 | 2221 | 4.77 | 6.75 | 1241 |

Source: Computed from Census of India 1971, 1981, Series-18, Rajasthan Part II-D, Migration Tables.

Table 4.7 gives us a comparative picture of in-migrants to Rajasthan from different states and out-migrants from Rajasthan to different states for 1971 and 1981 censuses.

The pattern of inter-state migration in Rajasthan for the periods 1971 and 1981 is more or less same. Following contingency tables 4.7 (A,B) of in-migrants to Rajasthan and out-migrants from Rajasthan show consistency in the pattern of migration.

The mean of the percentage of inmigrants (Table 4.7) to Rajasthan for 1971 and 1981 census is respectively (1.1139) and (1.2836). C.V. (196.39) and (187.29) show the high heterogeneity in the inter-state migration pattern of Rajasthan. The correlation coefficient (.96) shows the high temporal consistency in the regional pattern of in-migration of the state.

**TABLE 4.7**

**Percentage of Inmigrants in Rajasthan and Outmigrants from Rajasthan (Based on place of Birth in 1971, 1981)**

| S. No. | State/UT | Inmigrants 1971 | Inmigrants 1981 | Outmigrants 1971 | Outmigrants 1981 | Net Migration 1971 | Net Migration 1981 |
|---|---|---|---|---|---|---|---|
| 1 | 2 | 3 | 4 | 5 | 6 | 7 | 8 |
| 1. | Andhra Pradesh | 0.250 | 0.273 | 0.640 | 1.196 | - 0.440 | - 0.923 |
| 2. | Bihar | 0.948 | 1.329 | 0.567 | 0.052 | + .381 | + 1.277 |
| 3. | Gujarat | 5.678 | 3.139 | 8.672 | 11.840 | - 2.994 | - 8.701 |
| 4. | Haryana | 4.328 | 5.544 | 7.321 | 5.921 | - 2.993 | - 0.377 |
| 5. | Himachal Pradesh | 0.213 | 0.386 | 0.156 | 0.181 | + 0.057 | + 0.205 |
| 6. | Jammu & Kashmir | 0.144 | 0.244 | 0.112 | 0.146 | + 0.032 | + 0.098 |
| 7. | Karnataka | 0.258 | 0.305 | 0.201 | 0.278 | + 0.057 | + 0.027 |
| 8. | Kerala | 0.356 | 0.479 | 0.127 | 0.088 | + 0.229 | + 0.391 |
| 9. | Madhya Pradesh | 5.674 | 6.498 | 7.532 | 9.394 | - 1.859 | - 2.896 |
| 10. | Maharashtra | 0.783 | 1.864 | 0.653 | 0.789 | + 0.130 | + 1.075 |
| 11. | Manipur | 0.056 | 0.071 | 0.034 | 0.055 | + 0.022 | + 0.016 |
| 12. | Meghalaya | 0.019 | 0.028 | 0.076 | 0.089 | - 0.057 | - 0.061 |
| 13. | Nagaland | 0.016 | 0.026 | 0.030 | 0.035 | - 0.014 | - 0.009 |
| 14. | Orissa | 0.119 | 0.199 | 0.432 | 0.574 | - 0.313 | - 0.375 |
| 15. | Punjab | 6.434 | 7.455 | 5.344 | 3.292 | + 1.090 | + 4.163 |
| 16. | Sikkim | 0.002 | 0.028 | 0.029 | 0.038 | - 0.027 | - 0.010 |
| 17. | Tamil Nadu | 0.436 | 0.336 | 0.936 | 1.230 | - 0.500 | - 0.894 |

cont...

| 1 | 2 | 3 | 4 | 5 | 6 | 7 | 8 |
|---|---|---|---|---|---|---|---|
| 18. | Tripura | 0.005 | 0.033 | 0.136 | 0.023 | - 0.131 | + 0.010 |
| 19. | Uttar Pradesh | 7.382 | 8.786 | 3.416 | 2.856 | + 3.966 | + 5.930 |
| 20. | West Bengal | 0.312 | 0.913 | 1.156 | 3.180 | - 0.844 | - 2.267 |
| 21. | Andaman Nicobar | 0.004 | 0.002 | 0.006 | 0.005 | - 0.002 | - 0.003 |
| 22. | Arunachal Pradesh | 0.016 | 0.018 | 0.029 | 0.031 | - 0.013 | - 0.013 |
| 23. | Mizoram | 0.003 | 0.003 | 0.040 | 0.015 | - 0.037 | - 0.013 |
| 24. | Goa, Daman and Diu | 0.001 | 0.021 | 0.020 | 0.040 | - 0.019 | - 0.019 |
| 25. | Chandigarh | 0.090 | 0.065 | 0.563 | 0.330 | - 0.473 | - 0.265 |
| 26. | Dadar and Nagar Haveli | 0.003 | 0.001 | 0.004 | 0.006 | - 0.001 | - 0.005 |
| 27. | Delhi | 0.873 | 1.370 | 0.953 | 8.725 | - 0.080 | - 7.355 |
| 28. | Lakshadweep | — | — | — | — | — | — |
| 29. | Pondicherry | 0.01 | 0.001 | 0.001 | 0.001 | 0.000 | 0.000 |
| | Mean | 1.1139 | 1.2836 | 1.2846 | 1.6261 | - .1322 | - .3154 |
| | C.V. | 196.35 | 187.29 | 190.64 | 191.50 | | |
| | r | (.96) | | (.84) | | (.71) | |

Note: (a) The figures for Assam (outmigration) is not available in 1981 census due to disturbed conditions census could not be held in the state. For comparison the figures are also dropped from the 1971.

(b) Mean refers to the unweighted average of the 29 States/UTs included.

Source: Census of India, 1971, 1981—Migration Tables, D-Series, Part V.

The same trend is revealed by the Table 4.7(B) for outmigrants from Rajasthan. The respective means for the two censuses are (1.2846) and (1.6261). Again C.V. respectively (190.64) and (191.50) show the high variation for migration prevailing among the states. The correlation coefficient (.84) reflects the temporal consistency even in the regional pattern of out-migration from Rajasthan.

The states above average in 1971 and 1981 census, in both the Tables A and B are mainly bordered States of Rajasthan, except West Bengal in Table B for out-migration. It may be due to economic reasons. In 1981, Delhi has come up above average. It is the Capital of India and having more job opportunities than the State; with the increase in the percentage of educated people the negative effect of migration and distance is reduced to some extent.

In Table 4.7, a glance at net migration points out that outmigration from Rajasthan is more than in-migration. The mean value for net migration in 1961-71 is - .1322 while in 1981 it is - .3154. Net migration is calculated to find out whether a state is gainer or loser of its population. The high correlation coefficient (0.71) points out the consistency in net-migration for the periods under consideration 1971 and 1981.

**TABLE 4.7(A)**

**Distribution of States by Percentage of In-Migrations (1971, 1981)**

| | | 1981 | |
|---|---|---|---|
| | | *Below Average* | *Above Average 1971-81* |
| 1971 | Below Average | A.P., H.P., J & K, Karnataka, Kerala, Manipur, Meghalaya, Nagaland, Orissa, Sikkim, Tamilnadu, Tripura, West Bengal | Bihar, Maharashtra, Delhi |
| | Above average | Andaman Nicobar, Arunachal Pradesh, Mizoram, Goa, Chandigarh, Dadar Nagar Haveli, Lakshdweep, Pondicherry | Gujarat, Haryana MP, UP, Punjab |

Source: Based on Table 4.7.

**TABLE 4.7(B)**

**Distribution of States by Percentage of Out-Migrants (1971, 1981)**

| | | 1981 | |
|---|---|---|---|
| | | *Below Average* | *Above Average 1971-81* |
| 1971 | Below Average | A.P., H.P., J & K, Karnataka, Kerala, Manipur, Meghalaya, Nagaland, Orissa, Sikkim, Tamilnadu, Tripura, Mizoram Arunachal Pradesh, Goa, Chandigarh, Lakshdweep, Pondicherry | Bihar, Maharashtra, Delhi Andaman Nicobar, |
| | Above average | | Gujarat, Haryana MP, UP, Punjab West Bengal |

Source: Based on Table 4.7.

## REASONS FOR MIGRATION (1981)

In 1981 census, the scope of enquiry on migration has been widened further by collecting information on "reasons for migration" from *place of last residence* in addition to the enquiry made in 1971.

The reasons specified are—

(a) *Employment:* A person will have moved for employment in the following cases—

(i) If he/she has moved in search of a job or hoping to get a job.

(ii) Because he/she has got a job and has moved to take up the job.

(iii) Having already got a job, he/she has moved because of transfer, even if this is on promotion.

(b) *Education:* A person can be said to have moved for educational purpose if he/she has moved to the place of enumeration from his/her place of last residence for joining a school/college or any other type of educational institution either for the first time or for continuing his/her studies.

(c) *Family moved:* refers to the cases where the entire family moved with the Head of the family or the person on whom the family is dependent.

(d) *Marriage:* If a person moves from his/her last residence as a consequence of getting married.

(e) *Others:* will include all other reasons for migration, not covered by employment, education, family moved or marriage. This may include cases like movement due to retirement, movement for economic reasons such as to set up a shop or starting a business etc.

**TABLE 4.8**

**Percentage Distribution of All-Duration In-Migration in Accordance with Reasons for Migration, 1981**

(Based on *Duration of Residence*)

| *S.No.* | *Reasons* | *Total* | | | *Rural* | | | *Urban* | | |
|---|---|---|---|---|---|---|---|---|---|---|
| | | *Male* | *Female* | *Sex Ratio* | *Male* | *Female* | *Sex Ratio* | *Male* | *Female* | *Sex Ratio* |
| 1. | Employment | 39.08 | 1.89 | 162 | 33.30 | 1.45 | 248 | 48.42 | 3.62 | 103 |
| 2. | Education | 6.08 | 0.46 | 233 | 3.88 | 0.25 | 272 | 9.32 | 1.69 | 212 |
| 3. | Family Moved | 27.71 | 10.34 | 1224 | 27.73 | 7.08 | 1120 | 26.63 | 26.17 | 1388 |
| 4. | Marriage | 3.31 | 80.51 | 77144 | 4.51 | 84.69 | 83008 | 5.05 | 60.39 | 50487 |
| 5. | Others | 23.82 | 6.80 | 1019 | 30.58 | 6.53 | 1040 | 10.58 | 8.13 | |
| | Total | 100.00 | 100.00 | | 100.00 | 100.00 | | 100.00 | 100.00 | |

Source: Computed from Census of India, 1981, Series 18, Rajasthan Part II-D, Migration Tables.

Economic in-migration of males and demographic in-migration of females for marriage dominate among the reasons of in-migration. The severity of demographic in-migration is less in the urban areas. It is also clear from the sex ratios in Table 4.8.

Table 4.9 on next page shows both the male and female population is mobile for various reasons. This mobility decreases with the distances moved. Proportion of migrants (male and female) is the highest for intra-district (short distance) in-migration, least for inter-state (long-distance) and in between the two, is for inter-district (medium distance) in-migration. Sex ratio, in the Table 4.9, reveals main reasons for migration of male population are to get employment or to obtain education to improve their skill, whereas female migration is due to marriage and family moved reasons.

Premi (1989) studied pattern of internal migration in India and Rajasthan. According to him, employment, education, family moved, marriage etc. are the main reasons for migration. Employment as a reason for male life-time migration is more prominent in Rajasthan than in the country and intensity of employment as a reason for migration increased significantly from intra-district level to inter-state level. Education accounts for (6.1%) of the male migrants whereas in case of India, it is 5.2%. Among females, marriage is the most important reason, movement of the family is the second important reason for migration.

## 4.2 MIGRATION PATTERN IN DISTRICT LEVEL

On the basis of the data given in the Indian census, to highlight the regional variation of migration in Rajasthan, a study at the district level is also attempted.

Till 1961 census, question about place of last residence was not asked, so the studies were mainly concerned with migration into the place of enumeration from the place of

TABLE 4.9

**Percentage Distribution of All-Duration In-Migration in Different Distances with Reasons for Migration (1981)**

| S.No. | Migration Stream | Employment | | | Education | | | Family moved | | | Marriage | | | Others | | |
|---|---|---|---|---|---|---|---|---|---|---|---|---|---|---|---|---|
| | | Male | Female | Sex ratio | Male | Female | Sex ratio | Male | Female | Sex ratio | Male | Female | Sex ratio | Male | Female | Sex ratio |
| I | Intra-district | 47.53 | 49.55 | 155 | 59.85 | 42.33 | 182 | 52.67 | 42.99 | 1174 | 69.87 | 69.76 | 8260 | 57.71 | 61.49 | 972 |
| II | Inter-district | 30.94 | 29.83 | 144 | 29.01 | 32.54 | 288 | 25.75 | 38.44 | 1351 | 20.24 | 21.45 | 7803 | 27.62 | 26.57 | 992 |
| III | Inter-state | 21.53 | 20.63 | 143 | 11.14 | 25.13 | 558 | 21.58 | 18.57 | 1277 | 9.89 | 8.79 | 7183 | 14.67 | 11.94 | 763 |
| | | 100.00 | 100.00 | | 100.00 | 100.00 | | 100.00 | 100.00 | | 100.00 | 100.00 | | 100.00 | 100.00 | |

Source: Computed from Census of India, 1981, Series-18, Rajasthan, Part II-D, Migration Tables.

birth within the same district or the same state or India. So the district level cross-tabulation was not possible. 1971 census, for the first time made it possible to compute inter-district net-migration. The study relates to 26 districts of the state.[1]

**TABLE 4.10**

**Percentage Distribution of Lifetime In-Migrants to Population in 26 Districts of Rajasthan, 1971, 1981 (Based on Place of Birth)**

| *S. No.* | *District* | *In-migration as % of population* | | *Population (Sex Ratio)* | | *In-migration (Sex Ratio)* | |
|---|---|---|---|---|---|---|---|
| | | *1971* | *1981* | *1971* | *1981* | *1971* | *1981* |
| 1. | Sri Ganganagar | 43.77 | 42.70 | 874 | 874 | 1248 | 1290 |
| 2. | Bikaner | 25.78 | 25.96 | 901 | 891 | 2053 | 2284 |
| 3. | Churu | 25.43 | 25.90 | 946 | 953 | 4729 | 5328 |
| 4. | Jhunjhunu | 27.22 | 27.27 | 923 | 956 | 5423 | 5478 |
| 5. | Alwar | 28.54 | 22.54 | 887 | 892 | 3916 | 4550 |
| 6. | Bharatpur | 27.30 | 26.74 | 840 | 831 | 4625 | 5211 |
| 7. | Swai Madhopur | 28.37 | 21.19 | 864 | 866 | 4503 | 5567 |
| 8. | Jaipur | 28.82 | 29.04 | 890 | 893 | 3055 | 2740 |
| 9. | Sikar | 26.88 | 27.00 | 961 | 962 | 6598 | 7128 |
| 10. | Ajmer | 32.08 | 30.72 | 910 | 922 | 2532 | 2876 |
| 11. | Tonk | 28.95 | 28.47 | 909 | 927 | 1432 | 5137 |
| 12 | .Jaisalmer | 29.03 | 31.07 | 810 | 811 | 2717 | 2179 |
| 13. | Jodhpur | 25.30 | 23.85 | 900 | 909 | 2951 | 2999 |
| 14. | Nagaur | 27.17 | 27.05 | 942 | 957 | 4761 | 4355 |
| 15. | Pali | 30.79 | 31.59 | 950 | 946 | 3522 | 3356 |
| 16. | Barmer | 25.55 | 20.51 | 887 | 904 | 3442 | 3002 |
| 17. | Jalore | 27.05 | 27.56 | 931 | 941 | 4963 | 4278 |
| 18. | Sirohi | 32.60 | 31.94 | 957 | 963 | 2722 | 3377 |
| 19. | Bhilwara | 32.38 | 32.40 | 910 | 941 | 3828 | 4103 |

*(cont.)*

1. B.C. Mehta (1985) I.A.S.P. Paper

| S. No. | District | In-migration as % of population | | Population (Sex Ratio) | | In-migration (Sex Ratio) | |
|---|---|---|---|---|---|---|---|
| | | 1971 | 1981 | 1971 | 1981 | 1971 | 1981 |
| 20. | Udaipur | 29.41 | 25.94 | 957 | 977 | 4285 | 3213 |
| 21. | Chittorgarh | 33.43 | 38.48 | 930 | 951 | 4511 | 3228 |
| 22. | Dungarpur | 32.76 | 29.68 | 1015 | 1045 | 2247 | 4868 |
| 23. | Banswara | 22.39 | 27.68 | 978 | 984 | 4579 | 4028 |
| 24. | Bundi | 33.43 | 32.82 | 885 | 887 | 2266 | 2700 |
| 25. | Kota | 35.15 | 34.74 | 884 | 888 | 1889 | 1881 |
| 26. | Jhalawar | 30.79 | 29.04 | 919 | 926 | 3410 | 4092 |
| | Rajasthan | 29.76 | 29.80 | | | | |
| | Mean | 29.63 | 28.98 | | | | |
| | C.V. | 14.29 | 16.99 | | | | |
| | r | (.82) | | | | | |

Note: Mean refers to the unweighted average of 26 districts.
Source: Computed from Census of India 1971, 1981, Series-18, Rajasthan, Part II-D, Migration Tables.

Table 4.10 shows, some districts are having proportion of in-migrants of their population, above average, while in other districts this proportion is below average. Mehta (1983) has pointed out, migration is linked with development and prospective development of the district.

An individual moves to where his future appears most attractive or more formally to where he maximizes the present (discounted) value of future streams of benefits minus costs (opportunity, direct and psychic), subject to his limited knowledge of the world and its preferences." (Schultz; 1976).

It is clear from the Table 4.10, the coefficient of variation in 1971 is (14.29) which has increased to (16.99) in 1971-81, pointing to the growing regional variation in in-migration over the period. The pace of change is very slow, which is revealed by high correlation coefficient (.82) of 1971 and 1981.

This also shows the consistency in the pattern of in-migration of Rajasthan.

The overall sex ratio of total population of all the districts is less than 1,000 except Dungarpur district in both the periods 1971 and 1981. It may be due to the role economic out-migration of males.

From the sex ratio of inmigrants, it is clear that female in-migration is more than male in-migration in all the 26 districts.

**TABLE 4.10(A)**

**Distribution of Districts based on Percentage of In-Migrants (1971, 1981)**

| | *Below Average* | *Above Average 1971-81* |
|---|---|---|
| Below Average | Bikaner, Churu, Jhunjhunu, Alwar, Bharatpur, Swai Madhopur, Sikar, Tonk, Jodhpur, Nagaur, Barmer Jalore, Udaipur, Banswara | Jaipur, Jaisalmer |
| Above average | Dungarpur | Sri Ganganagar Ajmer, Pali, Sirohi, Bhilwara, Chittorgarh, Bundi, Kota, Jhalawar |

Source: Based on Table 4.10.

In contingency Table 4.10(A), districts are classified according to below and above average of the percentage of their inmigrants.

Except three districts of the State—Jaipur, Jaisalmer and Dungarpur—no change has occurred in the regional pattern of in-migration over the period under consideration.

Dungarpur has gone below the average of percentage of inmigrants whereas Jaipur and Jaisalmer have come upto the average.

Female in-migration is mainly due to marriage or family reasons. For the purpose of comparison of four migration streams for different distances in the Appendix Table A-4.1 only male inmigration is considered, which is mainly due to economic reasons.

From the Table A-4.1 (Appendix), it is clear that *rural to rural* male in-migration dominates in the short, medium and long distance. This percentage is less in inter-district in comparison to inter-state in-migration, as most of the states are contiguous states with the districts of the state. Their distance with the districts is less in comparison to inter-district distances. Rural to rural migration is mainly for economic. "It is directly related to the technological transformation of agriculture. A new technology or massive investment, as in the case of irrigation dams, is location specific. Successful adoption of a new (labour-using technology or investment in irrigation leads to a sharp shift in the demand for labour, which is not matched within a short period by an equal shift of supply of labour. The gap between the two and consequential rise in wages lead to movement of people from areas of low development to regions where rapid development takes place" (Shah & Patel; 1979).

Next in line comes, *rural to urban* in-migration. A glance at the Table A-4.1 (Appendix) shows for the medium distance (inter-district) it is higher than short and long distance in both the census periods 1971 and 1981. Rural to urban stream is regarded as a necessary concomitant of industrialization and modernization. In the view of some studies, the consequences of rural male out-migration are disturbing. "It has been observed that young and skilled population which is the change prone population, dominates the rural-urban migration stream. Therefore, this process deprives of the place of origin, of the potential work force. In such a mechanism, the backward areas (the place of origin) are left with traditional and dependent population and hence remain under-developed. The condition at the receiving end is also not very satisfactory. The process of rural male out-migration has been creating the problem of slum development and pressure on social amenities in big cities (Khan, 1981; Raza, 1977).

**TABLE 4.11**

**Mean, Coefficient of Variation and Correlation Coefficients of Four Migration Streams in 1971, 1981**

| | *Mean* | *C.V.* | *r* |
|---|---|---|---|
| INTRA DISTRICT | | | |
| 1971 R-R | 71.46 | 15.18 | |
| | | | (.52) |
| 1981 R-R | 62.63 | 25.54 | |
| 1971 U-R | 6.17 | 37.89 | |
| | | | (.77) |
| 1981 U-R | 6.43 | 37.12 | |
| 1971 R-U | 17.98 | 39.77 | |
| | | | (.82) |
| 1981 R-U | 22.51 | 34.77 | |
| 1971 U-U | 4.38 | 82.60 | |
| | | | (.88) |
| 1981 U-U | 5.59 | 60.94 | |
| INTER DISTRICT | | | |
| 1971 R-R | 43.63 | 28.53 | |
| | | | (.75) |

*(cont.)*

| | *Mean* | *C.V.* | *r* |
|---|---|---|---|
| 1981 | 43.48 | 43.28 | |
| R-R | | | |
| 1971 | 10.19 | 39.34 | |
| U-R | | | |
| | | | (.78) |
| 1981 | 9.57 | 33.28 | |
| U-R | | | |
| 1971 | 22.16 | 27.28 | |
| R-U | | | |
| | | | (.73) |
| 1981 | 24.88 | 38.87 | |
| R-U | | | |
| 1971 | 23.80 | 34.68 | |
| U-U | | | |
| | | | (.78) |
| 1981 | 22.26 | 31.29 | |
| U-U | | | |
| INTER STATE | | | |
| 1971 | 33.15 | 59.83 | |
| R-R | | | |
| | | | (.99) |
| 1981 | 32.83 | 73.97 | |
| R-R | | | |
| 1971 | 14.81 | 58.02 | |
| U-R | | | |
| | | | (.78) |
| 1981 | 14.53 | 50.98 | |
| U-R | | | |
| 1971 | 21.24 | 54.35 | |
| R-U | | | |
| | | | (.66) |
| 1981 | 21.23 | 67.19 | |
| R-U | | | |
| 1971 | 30.64 | 37.84 | |
| U-U | | | |
| | | | (.78) |
| 1981 | 31.09 | 48.30 | |
| U-U | | | |

Note: 1. Mean Refers to unweighted averge of 26 districts/
2. r is the correlation coefficient between migration streams of 1971 and 1981.

Lastly, comes *urban to urban* and *urban to rural* stream. The least is the urban to rural migration from the Table A-4.1 it is clear that the percentage of the urban to urban male migration is higher at the inter-district level and lowest at the intra-district level for all the 26 districts in the periods under consideration. From the social mobility point of view and of economic development, this may prove to be a healthy trend (Premi, 1983).

Table 4.11 shows at a glance the mean, coefficient of variation and correlation coefficient of four migration streams in all the distances for the census periods 1971 and 1981.

The coefficient of variation in the Table 4.11 shows the largest variation is prevailing in the urban to urban migration among the districts in the short distance in both the census period 1971 and 1981. It is respectively (82.60) and (60.94). In the medium distance, the largest variation is in the rural to rural migration stream for 1981. In the long distance, coefficient of variation is generally high in all the streams in comparison to intra-district and inter-district. This may be due to the reason that 17 out of 26 districts are bordered districts with other states. The co-efficient of correlation in the Table 4.11 shows the consistency in the twelve types of migration stream for the male in-migrants in the two periods 1971 and 1981. It is high in all the streams, except a little less (.52) for the rural to rural in-migration stream at the intra-district level. It may be due to the increase in the rural to urban in-migration or the balanced development of all the regions.

Table 4.12 shows at a glance inter-district lifetime net inmigration[1]. It points out the gainer and loser districts in view of migrants. It consists of the number of in-migrants minus the number of out-migrants and is the balance of a community or area.

---

1 Before 1971, it was not possible to compute net inter-district net migration.

**TABLE 4.12**

**Net Inter-District Migration in Rajasthan, 1971, 1981 (Place of Birth) (Males)**

| S. No. | Districts | Net Migration (1971) | Sex Ratio (In-migration) | Sex Ratio (Out-migration) | Net Migration 1981 | Sex Ratio (In-migration) | Sex Ratio (Out-migration) |
|---|---|---|---|---|---|---|---|
| 1. | Sri Ganganagar | + 3.70 | 1104 | 1939 | + 3.61 | 1101 | 1948 |
| 2. | Bikaner | - 0.74 | 1759 | 2309 | - 1.10 | 1819 | 2608 |
| 3. | Churu | - 1.27 | 5005 | 3073 | - 2.44 | 6410 | 3169 |
| 4. | Jhunjhunu | - 1.95 | 6434 | 2995 | - 2.50 | 6222 | 2841 |
| 5. | Alwar | - 1.07 | 5943 | 3486 | - 1.37 | 5370 | 3040 |
| 6. | Bharatpur | - 0.43 | 5238 | 2904 | - 1.03 | 5671 | 2466 |
| 7. | Swai Madhopur | - 0.21 | 3773 | 3588 | - 1.31 | 4642 | 3092 |
| 8. | Jaipur | + 1.15 | 2190 | 3602 | + 2.75 | 1989 | 3779 |
| 9. | Sikar | - 2.79 | 7730 | 3512 | - 3.28 | 2147 | 3441 |
| 10. | Ajmer | - 1.00 | 2495 | 2217 | - 1.85 | 2646 | 2215 |
| 11. | Tonk | - 0.52 | 4400 | 3019 | - 1.51 | 4630 | 2934 |
| 12. | Jaisalmer | - 3.37 | 1563 | 3005 | + 2.77 | 2042 | 3015 |
| 13. | Jodhpur | - 2.26 | 2124 | 2059 | - 1.51 | 4630 | 2934 |
| 14. | Nagaur | - 2.30 | 5253 | 2543 | - 3.42 | 5733 | 2416 |
| 15. | Pali | - 0.27 | 3047 | 2439 | + 0.40 | 2805 | 2644 |
| 16. | Barmer | + 0.20 | 2582 | 2773 | - 0.48 | 3008 | 2551 |
| 17. | Jalore | + 0.11 | 2842 | 3937 | + 0.72 | 2816 | 3553 |
| 18. | Sirohi | + 1.26 | 2195 | 2608 | + 1.48 | 2307 | 2845 |
| 19. | Bhilwara | + 0.27 | 3083 | 3426 | + 0.05 | 2966 | 2992 |
| 20. | Udaipur | - 0.51 | 3077 | 2969 | + 1.49 | 2590 | 2989 |
| 21. | Chittorgarh | + 2.63 | 2759 | 3397 | + 2.26 | 2141 | 2916 |
| 22. | Dungarpur | + 0.13 | 3544 | 3155 | - 1.96 | 3637 | 1524 |
| 23. | Banswara | + 0.31 | 1662 | 3459 | + 1.20 | 1672 | 2832 |
| 24. | Bundi | + 3.16 | 1660 | 2707 | + 3.65 | 1848 | 2899 |
| 25. | Kota | + 3.42 | 1271 | 2169 | + 4.40 | 1300 | 2446 |
| 26. | Jhalawar | - 0.90 | 2534 | 1970 | - 1.99 | 2888 | 1838 |

(r = .71)

Source: Computed from Census of India, 1971, 1981, Series-18 Rajasthan, Part II-D, Migration Tables.

Note: r is the correlation coefficient between net migration of 1971 and 1981.

In the state, there is large regional disparity in the inter-district out-migration and in-migration of males. From Table 4.12, it is clear that net result of migration streams between districts is significant only in few districts in 1971 and 1981. Sri Ganganagar leads the gainer with 3.70 per cent net in-migration in 1971. In 1981, this leading place goes to Kota with (4.40) net in-migration and Sri Ganganagar is on the second place with (3.61) net in-migrants. In the list of net losers i.e. with net out-migrants in 1971, Jaisalmer leads with 3.37 per cent out-migrants while in 1981 the place is shifted to Nagaur with 3.42 per cent out-migrants.

The following contingency Table 4.12(A) makes clear the losers and gainer districts in both the periods: 1971 and 1981.

**TABLE 4.12 (A)**

**Distribution of 26 Districts by Net Inter-District In-Migration (Males)**

| | | *1981* | |
|---|---|---|---|
| | | *LOSERS* | *GAINERS* |
| 1971 | LOSERS | Bikaner, Churu, Jhunjhunu, Alwar, Bharatpur, Swai Madhopur, Sikar, Ajmer, Tonk, Jodhpur, Nagaur Jhalawar | Jaisalmer Pali, Udaipur |
| | GAINERS | Barmer, Dungarpur | Sri Ganganagar, Jalore, Sirohi, Bhilwara, Chittorgarh, Banswara, Bundi, Kota |

Source: Based on Table 4.12

The coefficient of correlation (.71) between net migration of 1971 and 1981 shows the consistency in the pattern of net inter-district in-migration of the state for the two census periods 1971 and 1981.

## CONCLUSION

Migration is a permanent or semi-permanent change of residence. In Indian census 1971 onwards, data are collected in addition to place of birth on the basis of place of last residence. Migrants are classified into four streams based on rural and urban origin and rural and urban destination. They can also be classified according to distance moved i.e. short distance (intra-district), medium distance (inter-district) and long distance (inter-state). This study is conducted at two census periods, 1971 and 1981. There is consistency in the pattern of migration in the state. Female migration dominates in each and every stream. From the state, out-migration is more than in-migration. The contiguous bordered states of Rajasthan are having larger proportion in migratory movement of the state. Districts having borders with other states are having less share in inter-district population transactions. There is large regional variation in migratory process of the state. Developed districts have balanced their in and out migration, whereas the backward districts are still lagging behind. There should be a policy to develop these backward region, so that they should come up to the level of developed regions and thus there would be a balanced development of the state. The pattern of migration in Rajasthan is more or less same that of India.

In general, the migration pattern in Rajasthan conforms to the all-India pattern. The salient features of internal migration in India are as summarized below—

1. Migration in India is much smaller than in the western countries.
2. Bulk of migrants are females.
3. Rural to rural migration is a predominant feature of migration.

4. Rural to urban migration is generally a small proportion (nearly 15 per cent) of total migration.
5. Major proportion of migration (nearly 65 per cent) is short distance intra-district migration. Medium distance inter-district migration is relatively low at about 20 per cent of total migrants.
6. The principal purpose of migration is demographic for marriage or birth indicated by the relatively high sex-ratio (females per 1000 males).
7. Remigration and repeat migration as well as very short duration migration are quite frequent.
8. The sex-ratio decreases with distance moved. It is lower for urban origin and destination except in the case of urban to rural migration.
9. There is an inverse relation between distance to rural origin and rural destination (K.C. Zacharia; 1964; 1974. B.C. Mehta; 1988).

# 5

# *Inter-District Migration Linkages—1971, 1981*

Rajasthan is one of the largest states in India. Disparity in the state prevails in all the geographical, socio-economic characters. Due to this heterogeneity it is important to study the migration pattern in Rajasthan at district level.

Inter-state out, in and net migration have been the focus of the previous studies. Because upto 1961 census, questions about out-migration from the place of birth to other places within the state were not asked, only in-migration data were available. Since the name of the district of birth was not recorded, district level cross-tabulation was not possible and intra-district and inter-district flow of population could not be studied. 1971 census, for the first time, made it possible to compute an inter-district population transaction matrix for males and females from rural to rural, rural to urban, urban to rural and urban to urban places.

This Chapter describes the inter-district population transactions in three sections. Section 5.1 computes population transactions between districts in the state i.e. inter-district migration linkages are calculated.

Section 5.2 presents the results, identifies clusters of migration and correlates the same with clusters of socio-economic development. Section 5.3 concludes the Chapter. The study is focussed on inter-district population movements of male population, which is mainly for economic purpose. The female migration is for demographic reasons of marriage or child birth.

The Chapter IV—Pattern of Migration in Rajasthan—points out that there are large regional differentials in the inter-district out-migration, in-migration and so in the net-migration of males in both the census periods, 1971 and 1981.

Table 4.12-A in Chapter IV points out, Sri Ganganagar, Jalore, Sirohi, Bhilwara, Chittorgarh, Banswara, Bundi and Kota are the gainers, and Bikaner, Churu, Jhunjhunu, Alwar, Bharatpur, Swai Madhopur, Sikar, Ajmer, Tonk, Jodhpur, Nagaur and Jhalawar are the losers of population due to inter-regional population transactions. Jaisalmer, Pali, Udaipur are the gainers only in 1981 and Barmer, Dungarpur in 1971.

It can be hypothesized that the migrants make rational decision to select their place of residence. They migrate to the places where future prospects are brighter than the origin place. Distance from the source to destination area is the main intervening obstacle for the migrants. "Distance is the traditional proxy for migration costs" (Schultz). They prefer the places at the shorter distance instead of longer distance places. Short distance migration dominates in each and every stream of migration.

## 5.1 INTER-DISTRICT MIGRATION LINKAGES

On the basis of salient features of migration in Rajasthan, it is hypothesized that inter-district migration is confined to contiguous districts. In order to analyse inter-district population transactions, population transaction linkage matrix is computed for 26 districts and migration linkage coefficients is calculated for each district. The bilateral gross migration linkage between the two districts is given by Lij* -

---

*Kamble, N.D. (1983), Mehta, B.C. (1983)

$$Lij = \frac{1}{4}\left[\frac{Pij}{\frac{EiPi}{P}} + \frac{Pji}{\frac{EjPi}{P}} + \frac{Pij}{\frac{MjPi}{P}} + \frac{Pji}{\frac{MiPi}{P}}\right] \quad ...1$$

Where P = Total male population of Rajasthan = ΣPi

Pi = Male population of the ith district.

i = 1 to 26

Pij = Male population born in the ith district but enumerated in jth district, in-migrants to the jth district from ith district.

Ei = Total male out-migration from ith district

Mi = Total male in-migration in ith district

Ej = Total male out-migration from jth district

Mj = Total male in-migration in jth district.

When Lij is small, there is negligible population "transaction" between i & j districts. Lij = 1 denotes population transactions between the ith and jth districts in proportion to total in and out-migration of the two districts. If Lij = 1 for all j = 1, ..................26, it obviously means that district 1 has exactly proportionate population transactions with other districts. It is obvious that for a given i, neither can all Lij be less than 1 nor greater than 1. Larger a particular linkage Lij, greater is the gross migration between the two districts. The coefficient, however, does not show which district is the net gainer or net loser*.

There are two-way population movements between districts. Out migration of population from ith district to jth district (Pij) is in-migration from the point of view of jth district. The size of migrants should, therefore, be normalized with respect to the population of the two districts. The terms in the formulae can be interpreted as follows :

---

* [This is a limitation of the coefficient since it is based on the gross rather than the net migration and ignore the direction of migration].

$$\frac{Pij/Ei}{Pj/P} = \frac{\text{Share of out-migration from i to j in total out-migration from ith}}{\text{jth districts relative pull}}$$

and

$$\frac{Pij/Mj}{Pi/P} = \frac{\text{ith district's share in the total in-migrant population of the jth district}}{\text{ith district's relative push}}$$

Similarly, the other two terms can also be explained. If the relative shares are in proportion to their respective population shares, then all these terms will be equal to 1 and Lij will also be 1. Obviously, since Lij = Lji, the linkage matrix is symmetric.

## 5.2 RESULTS INTER-REGIONAL POPULATION TRANSACTION

Inter-regional population transaction linkages between all the 26 districts in Rajasthan for 1971 and 1981, on the basis of male migration stream, are presented in this Section. The results for 1971 have been computed by Mehta (1983)[1] and given in Table 5.1.

On the basis of inter-regional population transaction

---

Normalization with respect to the total in and out migrants, without considering the total population of the transacting districts can also be considered. Then the linkage measure would be -

$$Lij' = \frac{1}{4}\left[\frac{Pij}{Ei} + \frac{Pji}{Ej} + \frac{Pij}{Mj} + \frac{Pji}{Mi}\right] \ldots 2$$

Lij′ will also be non-negative. However, this index can exceed unity. Moreover, no value of Lij, similar to the bench mark value of Lij = 1 in formula (1), can be chosen. Formula (1) is obviously superior to formula (2), since a mere inspection of the Lij matrix derived from it will tell us whether the gross migration of a particular district to and from other districts is uniformly distributed or not.

1. B.C. Mehta (1983), IASP Paper

**TABLE 5.1**

**Inter-district Migration Linkages (1971)**

| S. No. District | 1 | 2 | 3 | 4 | 5 | 6 | 7 | 8 | 9 | 10 | 11 | 12 | 13 | 14 | 15 | 16 | 17 | 18 | 19 | 20 | 21 | 22 | 23 | 24 | 25 | 26 |
|---|---|---|---|---|---|---|---|---|---|---|---|---|---|---|---|---|---|---|---|---|---|---|---|---|---|---|
| 1. Sri Ganganagar | - | 11.01 | 5.93 | 1.74 | 0.46 | 0.15 | 0.09 | 0.64 | 1.18 | 0.26 | 0.05 | 2.36 | 1.21 | 0.86 | 0.19 | 0.43 | 0.14 | 0.28 | 0.22 | 0.01 | 0.07 | 0.04 | 0.14 | 0.23 | 0.26 | 0.05 |
| 2. Bikaner | | | 7.50 | 1.31 | 0.49 | 0.24 | 0.16 | 3.49 | 1.14 | 0.40 | 0.12 | 5.19 | 2.34 | 3.41 | 0.49 | 0.71 | 0.16 | 0.22 | 0.18 | 0.28 | 0.09 | 0.05 | 0.21 | 0.11 | 0.27 | 0.10 |
| 3. Churu | | | | 4.54 | 0.18 | 0.12 | 0.09 | 0.28 | 3.60 | 0.26 | 0.02 | 0.54 | 0.68 | 1.83 | 0.14 | 0.15 | 0.03 | 0.08 | 0.06 | 0.08 | 0.04 | 0.13 | 0.20 | 0.14 | 0.12 | 0.08 |
| 4. Jhunjhunu | | | | | 0.63 | 0.28 | 0.49 | 2.34 | 4.92 | 0.68 | 1.16 | 0.25 | 0.40 | 0.92 | 0.99 | 0.22 | 0.06 | 0.08 | 0.55 | 0.21 | 0.15 | 0.04 | 0.02 | 0.09 | 0.18 | 0.10 |
| 5. Alwar | | | | | | 4.23 | 0.80 | 3.22 | 1.81 | 0.86 | 0.81 | 0.29 | 0.64 | 0.33 | 0.11 | 0.23 | 0.12 | 0.17 | 0.40 | 0.21 | 0.07 | 0.04 | 0.06 | 0.16 | 0.33 | 0.08 |
| 6. Bharatpur | | | | | | | 2.88 | 1.13 | 0.21 | 0.81 | 0.14 | 0.75 | 0.37 | 0.15 | 0.18 | 0.15 | 0.09 | 0.15 | 0.07 | 0.33 | 0.16 | 0.10 | 0.08 | 0.12 | 0.46 | 0.17 |
| 7. Swai Madhopur | | | | | | | | 1.56 | 0.42 | 0.51 | 3.72 | 0.25 | 0.17 | 0.17 | 0.06 | 0.12 | 0.10 | 0.06 | 0.14 | 0.17 | 0.08 | 0.18 | 0.18 | 1.45 | 3.53 | 0.59 |
| 8. Jaipur | | | | | | | | | 2.23 | 2.88 | 3.19 | 0.39 | 1.10 | 1.35 | 0.31 | 0.23 | 0.15 | 0.74 | 0.41 | 0.47 | 0.22 | 0.19 | 0.22 | 0.58 | 0.89 | 0.28 |
| 9. Sikar | | | | | | | | | | 0.72 | 0.23 | 0.63 | 0.35 | 2.43 | 0.07 | 0.26 | 0.15 | 0.14 | 0.33 | 0.16 | 0.07 | 0.11 | 0.10 | 0.13 | 0.31 | 0.13 |
| 10. Ajmer | | | | | | | | | | | 2.64 | 0.30 | 1.17 | 2.32 | 3.04 | 0.92 | 0.24 | 2.00 | 4.76 | 1.51 | 1.12 | 0.33 | 0.33 | 1.12 | 1.43 | 0.28 |
| 11. Tonk | | | | | | | | | | | | 0.10 | 0.45 | 1.05 | 0.27 | 0.06 | 0.19 | 0.29 | 2.33 | 0.34 | 0.72 | 0.37 | 0.06 | 11.41 | 5.29 | 0.75 |
| 12. Jaisalmer | | | | | | | | | | | | | 8.45 | 1.03 | 0.93 | 11.54 | 0.46 | 0.20 | 0.11 | 0.30 | 0.05 | 0.13 | 0.08 | 0.11 | 0.13 | 0.04 |
| 13 Jodhpur | | | | | | | | | | | | | | 4.43 | 5.29 | 6.95 | 2.57 | 1.43 | 0.81 | 0.64 | 0.28 | 0.20 | 0.33 | 1.84 | 0.56 | 0.09 |
| 14 Nagaur | | | | | | | | | | | | | | | 1.64 | 0.68 | 0.34 | 0.34 | 0.23 | 0.13 | 0.14 | 0.01 | 0.38 | 0.20 | 00.31 | 0.07 |
| 15 Pali | | | | | | | | | | | | | | | | 1.60 | 4.90 | 7.80 | 0.68 | 1.78 | 0.38 | 0.11 | 0.04 | 0.32 | 0.48 | 0.14 |
| 16 Barmer | | | | | | | | | | | | | | | | | 9.58 | 0.92 | 0.03 | 0.09 | 0.12 | 0.05 | - | 0.16 | 0.10 | 0.06 |
| 17 Jalore | | | | | | | | | | | | | | | | | | 9.81 | 0.06 | 0.08 | 0.14 | 0.02 | - | 0.16 | 0.10 | 0.05 |
| 18 Sirohi | | | | | | | | | | | | | | | | | | | 0.28 | 2.32 | 0.47 | 0.38 | 0.06 | 0.42 | 0.24 | 0.04 |
| 19 Bhilwara | | | | | | | | | | | | | | | | | | | | 3.59 | 4.25 | 0.12 | 0.47 | 3.72 | 0.75 | 0.30 |
| 20 Udaipur | | | | | | | | | | | | | | | | | | | | | 6.42 | 8.12 | 2.48 | 0.71 | 0.52 | 0.26 |
| 21 Chittorgarh | | | | | | | | | | | | | | | | | | | | | | 1.56 | 3.61 | 0.68 | 2.13 | 0.87 |
| 22 Dungarpur | | | | | | | | | | | | | | | | | | | | | | | 1.56 | 3.61 | 0.68 | 0.99 |
| 23 Banswara | | | | | | | | | | | | | | | | | | | | | | | | 0.36 | 0.42 | 0.11 |
| 24 Bundi | | | | | | | | | | | | | | | | | | | | | | | | | 13.19 | 1.76 |
| 25 Kota | | | | | | | | | | | | | | | | | | | | | | | | | | 12.60 |
| 26 Jhalawar | | | | | | | | | | | | | | | | | | | | | | | | | | |

Source : Computed by the author from Census of India, 1971, Series 18, Rajasthan, Part II-D, Migration Tables.

linkages coefficients, he has identified five clusters of close linkages:

| | |
|---|---|
| Cluster 1: | Sri Ganganagar, Bikaner, Churu, Jhunjhunu (Jaipur, Sikar, Jaisalmer, Jodhpur, Tonk and Nagaur). |
| Cluster 2: | Alwar, Bharatpur, Swai Madhopur, Jaipur, Sikar, Ajmer and tonk (Jodhpur, Nagaur, Pali, Sirohi, Bhilwara, Udaipur, Chittorgarh, Bundi and Kota). |
| Cluster 3: | Jaisalmer, Jodhpur, Nagaur, Pali, Barmer, Jalore, Sirohi (Udaipur, Bundi) |
| Cluster 4: | Bhilwara, Udaipur, Chittorgarh, Dungarpur, and Banswara (Bundi, Kota). |
| Cluster 5: | Bundi, Kota and Jhalawar. |

Note: Districts placed in brackets can be put more in than one cluster.

On the basis of Mehta (1983) study, migration linkages coefficients are calculated for 1981 in Table 5.2.

Table 5.2 indicates broadly the same five clusters as were identified by Mehta. While observing the marked values outside the clusters, some changes are visible from 1971 but they are negligible. The negative signs are assigned in Table 5.2 by comparing the Pij values (out-migration of both the ith and jth districts). Negative signs represent out-migration of jth district to ith district is more than ith to jth district.

These five clusters support the formulated hypothesis that most of the inter-district population transactions are confined to contiguous districts.

The linkages values marked outside the cluster in Table 5.1 for 1971 and in Table 5.2 for 1981, indicate that Bikaner of Cluster-1 has substantial linkages outside the cluster e.g. Jaipur, Sikar and Tonk of Cluster-2 and Jaisalmer, Jodhpur and Nagaur

**TABLE 5.2**

**Inter-district Migration Linkages (1981)**

| *S. No.* | *District* | *1* | *2* | *3* | *4* | *5* | *6* | *7* | *8* | *9* | *10* | *11* | *12* | *13* | *14* | *15* | *16* | *17* | *18* | *19* | *20* | *21* | *22* | *23* | *24* | *25* | *26* |
|---|---|---|---|---|---|---|---|---|---|---|---|---|---|---|---|---|---|---|---|---|---|---|---|---|---|---|---|
| 1. | Sri Ganganagar | | -10.08 | -5.21 | -2.00 | -0.66 | -0.20 | -0.10 | -0.55 | -1.40 | -0.25 | -1.40 | -1.23 | -0.95 | -1.21 | 0.13 | 0.50 | 0.15 | 0.09 | 0.07 | 0.09 | 0.03 | 0.03 | 0.04 | 0.23 | 0.25 | 0.02 |
| 2. | Bikaner | | | -6.59 | -1.03 | -0.32 | -0.16 | -0.09 | -0.69 | -0.84 | -0.38 | -0.06 | 4.79 | -2.10 | 3.15 | 0.37 | 0.49 | 0.13 | 0.28 | 0.10 | 0.25 | 0.05 | 0.04 | 0.11 | 0.11 | 0.23 | 0.04 |
| 3. | Churu | | | | -4.01 | 0.34 | 0.10 | -0.13 | 0.48 | -2.76 | 0.11 | 0.03 | -0.47 | -0.34 | 1.97 | 0.19 | 0.08 | 0.06 | 0.01 | 0.07 | 0.07 | 0.04 | 0.05 | 0.05 | 0.10 | 0.17 | 0.03 |
| 4. | Jhunjhunu | | | | | 0.69 | 0.44 | 0.45 | 1.75 | -6.79 | 0.54 | 0.30 | 0.23 | 0.29 | 0.52 | 0.12 | 0.09 | 0.06 | 0.09 | 0.20 | 0.15 | 0.12 | 0.11 | 0.18 | 0.14 | 0.25 | 0.06 |
| 5. | Alwar | | | | | | -5.01 | -1.15 | 3.15 | 0.67 | 0.74 | 0.22 | 0.18 | 0.25 | 0.27 | 0.15 | 0.17 | 0.09 | 0.23 | 0.17 | 0.22 | 0.12 | 0.09 | 0.15 | 0.17 | 0.29 | 0.11 |
| 6. | Bharatpur | | | | | | | -3.27 | -1.40 | 0.26 | 0.55 | 0.29 | 0.21 | -0.29 | 0.20 | 0.15 | 0.10 | 0.17 | 0.10 | 0.10 | 0.19 | 0.17 | 0.18 | 0.28 | 0.31 | 0.79 | 0.30 |
| 7. | Swai Madhopur | | | | | | | | 2.28 | -0.23 | 0.52 | 3.49 | 0.08 | -0.20 | 0.19 | 0.07 | 0.09 | 0.20 | 0.18 | 0.15 | 0.18 | 0.13 | 0.04 | 0.23 | 1.73 | 3.05 | 0.73 |
| 8. | Jaipur | | | | | | | | | -2.98 | -2.71 | -3.16 | -0.17 | -0.81 | 1.38 | 0.40 | 0.16 | 0.20 | 0.64 | 0.52 | 0.56 | 0.22 | 0.22 | 0.35 | 0.48 | 0.86 | 0.28 |
| 9. | Sikar | | | | | | | | | | 0.64 | 0.44 | 1.23 | 0.25 | 2.49 | 0.25 | 0.09 | 0.07 | 0.25 | 0.41 | 0.16 | 0.07 | 0.09 | 0.21 | 0.12 | 0.17 | 0.09 |
| 10. | Ajmer | | | | | | | | | | | 3.52 | -0.18 | 1.04 | 2.81 | 3.67 | 0.50 | 0.24 | 1.78 | 4.63 | 1.54 | 0.94 | 0.62 | 0.48 | 1.31 | 1.33 | 0.26 |
| 11. | Tonk | | | | | | | | | | | | 0.04 | -0.11 | 0.27 | 0.13 | 0.07 | 0.12 | 0.12 | 1.34 | 0.09 | 0.26 | 0.15 | 0.21 | 5.08 | 2.71 | 0.41 |
| 12. | Jaisalmer | | | | | | | | | | | | | -8.96 | 0.80 | 0.54 | 13.78 | 0.80 | 0.35 | 0.11 | 0.22 | 0.11 | 0.05 | 0.07 | 0.09 | 0.19 | 0.06 |
| 13. | Jodhpur | | | | | | | | | | | | | | 3.97 | 5.04 | 5.13 | 2.65 | 1.20 | 0.22 | 0.53 | 0.21 | 0.09 | 0.29 | 0.31 | 0.49 | 0.08 |
| 14. | Nagaur | | | | | | | | | | | | | | | 1.50 | 0.51 | 0.31 | 0.27 | 0.22 | 0.19 | 0.17 | 0.07 | 0.22 | 0.24 | 0.26 | 0.14 |
| 15. | Pali | | | | | | | | | | | | | | | | 1.74 | 4.56 | 7.74 | 0.75 | 1.84 | 0.70 | 0.27 | 0.53 | 0.14 | 0.34 | 0.26 |
| 16. | Barmer | | | | | | | | | | | | | | | | | 9.54 | 0.63 | 0.10 | 0.14 | 0.22 | 0.02 | 0.10 | 0.07 | 0.12 | 0.20 |
| 17. | Jalore | | | | | | | | | | | | | | | | | | 9.22 | 0.07 | 0.16 | 0.11 | 0.02 | 0.12 | 0.04 | 0.09 | 0.04 |
| 18. | Sirohi | | | | | | | | | | | | | | | | | | | 0.34 | 2.72 | 0.25 | 0.22 | 0.03 | 0.18 | 0.15 | 0.09 |
| 19. | Bhilwara | | | | | | | | | | | | | | | | | | | | 3.27 | 6.55 | 0.21 | 0.31 | 4.06 | 0.80 | 0.44 |
| 20. | Udaipur | | | | | | | | | | | | | | | | | | | | | 6.54 | 6.22 | 2.85 | 0.52 | 0.47 | 0.28 |
| 21. | Chittorgarh | | | | | | | | | | | | | | | | | | | | | | 0.53 | 3.65 | 1.22 | 2.51 | 1.62 |
| 22. | Dungarpur | | | | | | | | | | | | | | | | | | | | | | | 19.18 | 0.03 | 0.10 | 0.12 |
| 23. | Banswara | | | | | | | | | | | | | | | | | | | | | | | | 0.28 | 1.33 | 0.48 |
| 24. | Bundi | | | | | | | | | | | | | | | | | | | | | | | | | 11.55 | 2.38 |
| 25. | Kota | | | | | | | | | | | | | | | | | | | | | | | | | | 11.59 |
| 26. | Jhalawar | | | | | | | | | | | | | | | | | | | | | | | | | | — |

Source : Computed from Census of India, 1981, Series 18, Rajasthan, Part II-D, Migration Tables.

of Cluster-3. Sikar of Cluster-2 has substantial linkages with all the districts of Cluster-1. Sri Ganganagar is linked with Jaisalmer and Jodhpur of Cluster-3 and Jhunjhunu with Tonk of Cluster-2.

Nagaur of Cluster-3 has linkages with Jaipur, Sikar and Ajmer of Cluster-2. Ajmer has also linkages with Jodhpur, Sirohi, Bhilwara, Udaipur, Banswara, Bundi and Kota. Swai Madhopur is also linked with Bundi and Kota.

In the Cluster-3, Udaipur of Cluster-4 is having linkages with Pali and Sirohi whereas Bundi of Cluster-5 with Jodhpur.

In the Cluster-4, Bhilwara and Dungarpur have significant transactions with Bundi of Cluster-5. Bundi has highly diffused population transactions with other districts in the State.

Thus Bikaner, Jodhpur, Sikar and Nagaur which are all in the arid and semi-arid region and have substantial Jat population and cultural similarity have substantial linkages outside the clusters. Ajmer is centrally located, hence has widely diffused linkages.

Intra-cluster linkages are very strong in Cluster-5 and 1, all Lij being larger than unity. They are culturally homogeneous clusters and are composed of contiguous and climatically and geo-physically similar districts.

Cluster-2 consists of 7 districts in the plain regions. It is the most heterogeneous cluster, as many as 10 out of 21 Lijs are less than unity. Ajmer is the weakest link which can be placed in Cluster-3 or Cluster-4 and so Sikar in Cluster-1.

In Cluster-3, out of 21 only 7 Lij's are less than one. This is also a culturally and geo-physically homogeneous group. Cluster-4 is also strongly inter-linked, with only 2 out of 10 values are less than unity.

Following map of Rajasthan shows at a glance 26 districts

of the state classified into five clusters of inter-district population movements in 1971 and 1981.

Mehta (1978; 15-19) clustered 26 districts of Rajasthan into homogeneous groups on the basis of various indicators of socio-economic development. On the basis of this study (Mehta; 1978), Jaisalmer, Barmer and Jalore are the lowest developed districts followed by a cluster of two districts, Dungarpur and Banswara, and another cluster of Jhunjhunu, Sikar, Nagaur and Churu. A cluster of four districts, Alwar, Kota, Bharatpur and Pali is of relatively medium developed districts. And the most developed districts i.e. Sri Ganganagar, Jodhpur, Bikaner, Ajmer and Jaipur form single district clusters independent of each other.

Thus Mehta (1978; 17) points out "this leads to the interesting result that development is isolated but under-development is in clusters. That means higher development of some districts may be due to some special historical and other factors, whereas under-development is due to geo-physical and other structural factors.... The most developed districts are surrounded by very slowly developed districts except Jaipur."

While looking at the migration clusters and development clusters, it is interesting to note that each migration Cluster consists of some districts from low and medium development clusters and one or two districts from high development clusters. In the migration Cluster-1, four districts, Jhunjhunu, Sikar, Nagaur and Churu are from less developed cluster and Sri Ganganagar and Bikaner are from high development clusters. In migration Cluster-2, Jaisalmer, Barmer and Jalore are from the lowest development cluster and Jodhpur and Ajmer are from the highest development clusters. In Cluster-3, Jaipur, the most developed district, is surrounded by Alwar, Bharatpur, Tonk and Swai Madhopur, least developed districts. In Cluster-4, Dungarpur and Banswara are the least developed

MAP

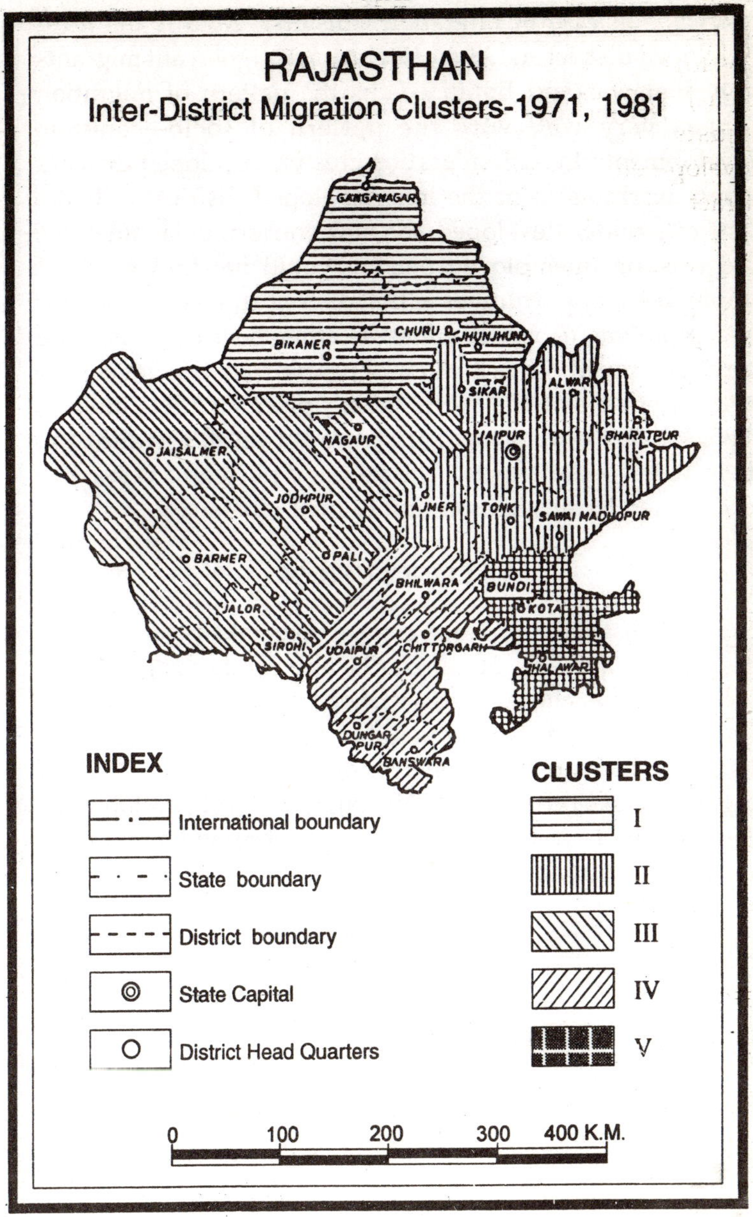

RAJASTHAN
Inter-District Migration Clusters-1971, 1981
GANGANAGAR
BIKANER
CHURU
JHUNJHUNU
SIKAR
ALWAR
BHARATPUR
JAIPUR
NAGAUR
JAISALMER
JODHPUR
AJMER
TONK
SAWAI MADHOPUR
BARMER
PALI
BHILWARA
BUNDI
KOTA
JALOR
SIROHI
UDAIPUR
CHITTORGARH
JHALAWAR
DUNGARPUR
BANSWARA
INDEX
International boundary
State boundary
District boundary
State Capital
District Head Quarters
CLUSTERS
I
II
III
IV
V
0 100 200 300 400 K.M.

and Bhilwara, Chittorgarh and Udaipur are medium developed districts. In case of migration Cluster-5, Kota is the most developed district and, therefore, attracts significant migrants from Jhalawar and Bundi. Thus the pattern of migration adjusts very well with the pattern of socio-economic development. In each migration cluster, developed districts attract migrants from the less developed districts. "If the district is under-developed, the new entrants in labour-force and existing unemployed persons could not find much of employment opportunities in that district and would look for the employment opportunities in other districts which are fairly developed. Thus the flow of people from less developed to developed districts starts taking place." (A.K. Gumber; 1985, 35). The developed districts are not yet able to diffusion their wide-spread effects. The pull and push effects seem to be confined to intra-cluster, not to inter-clusters.

## 5.3 CONCLUSION

Inter-district population transactions take place more or less with in a cluster of geographically contiguous districts. Each migration cluster consists of one or two relatively more developed districts having possibly a pull effect on the other districts which are relatively less developed. The pattern of migration clusters fits very well into the pattern of development. The migration streams are, however, confined within the respective clusters.

# 6

# *Migration Models— At District Level (1971, 1981)*

To determine some of the forces that affect migration, statistical regression models are estimated for male population. The male selective migration is largely attributed to economic reasons and to pursue higher education; the female migration, a dominating scene in an exagomous society is attributed to social practice of kinship development (Premi & Rathore; 1986).

This chapter is divided into four sections. In Section 6.1 model is specified and the variables included in the model are introduced with their names and definitions. In Section 6.2 hypotheses are formulated on the basis of past studies and generalisations. In Section 6.3, hypothesis are tested by performing step by step regression analysis in both the census periods 1971 and 1981. Results are presented in this Section. The models are also estimated for the pooled data for 1971 and 1981. As the pooling increases, the accuracy of estimates (Hannan and Young; 1977).

Section 6.3 is further sub-divided into sub-sections. 6.3A deals with decadal district in-migration (male) model. In 6.3B, decadal district in-migration (male) excluding intra-district in-migration (male) is discussed. Sub-section 6.3C deals with rural to rural decadal district in-migration (male) model. In 6.3D rural to urban decadal district in-migration model is analysed. And the last sub-section 6.3E is related with net inter-district migration. Sub-section 6.4 concluded the chapter.

Section 6.3 is further sub-divided into sub-sections. Each sub-section is concerned with the different dependent variable while independent variables remaining the same.

## 6.1 SPECIFICATION OF THE MODEL AND SUMMARY OF THE VARIABLES

To test the implications of the theory in the present study, only single equation linear structural model is specified. The regression model is of the usual form.

$$Mi = b_1 + b_2 x_{i2} + b_3\ xi_3 ...... + bnxi_n + e_i$$
$$(i = 1, 2, ........................26)$$

$X_i$'s are independent variables, Mi is dependent variable and b's are the regression coefficients, ei is the disturbance term. The model is assumed to conform to the standard assumptions of classical linear regression model.

The summary of the variables used in subsequent models is given in Table 6.1.

**TABLE 6.1**

**Summary of Variables used in District Migration Models**

| *S. No.* | *Explanatory* | *Acronym (X's)* | *Definition of variables* |
|---|---|---|---|
| 1 | 2 | 3 | 4 |
| 1. | Density of population[1] | (DP) | Persons living per sq km of area. |
| 2. | Centres of Administration | (CA) | Number of capital towns in each district is taken from the general population tables. |
| 3. | Prospects of Development | (PD) | Per capita plan expenditure in districts (in rupees). |

*cont...*

| 1 | 2 | 3 | 4 |
|---|---|---|---|
| 4. | Distance | (D) | In kms of the District Headquarters from the nearest two cities. Distance is taken from the shortest road routes. |
| 5. | Degree of Urbanisation | (DU) | $\frac{\text{Total urban population of the ith district}}{\text{Total population of the ith district}} \times 100$ |
| 6. | Livestock | (LIV) | Per hectare of net sown area — $\frac{\text{Total number of livestock}}{\text{Net sown area}}$ |
| 7. | Agricultural Labourer | (AL) | Percentage of agricultural labourer to total workers for each district. Data have been taken from population census reports of relevant years. |
| 8. | Migrant stock | (SMR) | the number of migrants located in district j, who migrated from place i in the period before the census period of 10 years i.e. people living in district j above 10 years, divided by the population of the district. |
| 9. | Average age of the population | (AA) | the weighted average of people in various 5 years age groups, using the median of each group weighted by the number of people in the group and summed over all groups and divided by total population for each district. The oldest group is open-intervalled and arbitrarily chosen median is to be 60 years. Nine *composite indices* are constructed in this study. |

*cont...*

| 1 | 2 | 3 | 4 |
|---|---|---|---|
| | | | Wherever, there are two indicators, equal weightage method has been adopted otherwise principal component analysis and the first principal component which explains the largest variation is considered in this study for 1971 and 1981 census periods. |
| 10. | Medical Facilities | (MF) | composite of (a) total number of hospital beds and (b) doctors per lakh population. The percentage of total variance explained by first principal component in these two variables in 75 per cent in 1971 & 70 per cent in 1981. |
| 11. | Transport Index | (TP) | includes (a) roads; and (b) railways per 10,000 sq km. of area. 85 per cent variance in the two variables is explained by the first principal component in 1971 & 80 per cent in 1981. |
| 12. | Index of Social Backwardness | (SB) | includes percentage of (a) Schedule Caste; and (b) Scheduled Tribe to the total population as given in the census. The first principal component explains 80 per cent of the total variance in the included variables in 1971 & 82 per cent in 1981. |
| 13. | Banking and Credit | (BAC) | combination of total (a) number of commercial banks per lakh population and (b) loans advanced by cooperative societies per hectare of gross cropped area. First principal component explains 85 per cent of the total variance in these two original variables in 1971 & 70 per cent in 1981. |

*cont...*

| 1 | 2 | 3 | 4 |
|---|---|---|---|
| 14. | Education Index | (ED) | composite of (a) percentage of literates to total population (b) percentage of literates with some schooling and (c) total number of educational institutions per lakh population. The first principal component accounts for 61.21 per cent variance of the total variance in the orginal variables in 1971 & 69.52 per cent in 1981. |
| 15. | Index of Industrial Development | (ID) | aggregation of four indicators (a) ratio of total number of registered factories in the ith district to the total number of registered factories, (b) % of workers in manufacturing industries to total workers, (c) per capita value added in manufacturing and (d) per capita capital employed in manufacturing industries. First principal component explains in 1971, 72.44 per cent variance of the total variance in these four indicators and 85 per cent of variance in 1981. |
| 16. | Mechanization in Agriculture Index | (MECA) | combination of three indicators (a) pumps + oil engines in per 1000 hectare, (b) tractors per 1000 hectare of net sown area, and (c) power consumption in agriculture per hectare of gross cropped area. The percentage of total variance explained by first principal component in these three indicators in 1971 is 62.06 per cent and in 1981 61.33 per cent. |
| 17. | Water Resource Index | (WR) | composite of six indicators- (a) consumption of fertilizers per ten hectare of gross cropped area, (b) percentage share of wells and |

*cont...*

| 1 | 2 | 3 | 4 |
|---|---|---|---|
| | | | tubewells in irrigation, (c) normal rainfall in cms., (d) irrigation extent, (e) cropping intensity, and (f) irrigation intensity. The percentage of the total variation explained by first principal component in these six original variables is 36.42 per cent in 1971 and 40.48 per cent in 1981. |
| 18. | Agricultural Output Index | (AO) | aggregation of four indicators (a) land productivity, (b) labour productivity, (c) commercialisation, and (d) per capita availability of foodgrains. First principal component accounts for 46.40 per cent of the total variance in these four indicaotrs in 1971 and explain 46.93 per cent of the variance in 1981. |
| 19. | District Dummy Variable | DV districts | DV = 0 for border and DV=1 for non-border districts. |
| 20. | Temporal Dummy Variable | DVT | DVT= 0 for the base year 1971 and DVT=1 for the year 1981 model. |

1. Population is not included as an explanatory variable in the regression model, the reason being its presumed endogeneity. Today's population is in large part determined by past migration flows. Like today's migration decision, past periods' migration decisions were themselves determined by past economic conditions. Since in a particular labour market, current economic conditions tend to be highly correlated with previous period's conditions (see Mincer, 1966; Hall, 1970), etc), ordinary least squares estimation of a migration model including population as an exogenous explanatory variable would produce inconsistent regression coefficients. Fields, G.S. (1979) "Place to place Migration : Some new Evidence", *The Review of Economics & Statistics*, Vol. LXI, No.1.

Thus the variables affecting the migratory movements is a combination of economic, sociological, demographic and political variables. The set of explanatory variables is common to all models.

**Dependent Variables** relate to male population of the district for 1971 and 1981 census periods.

| *S. No.* | *Dependent (Y's)* | *Acronym* | *Definition of variables* |
|---|---|---|---|
| 1. | Decadal district in-migration rate | DM | $\frac{\text{Decadal male in-migrants of the ith district}}{\text{Total male population of the ith district}}$ |
| 2. | Decadal district in-migration rate excluding intra-district in-migration. | DME | $\frac{\text{Decadal male in-migrants of the ith district less male intra-district in-migrants}}{\text{Total male population of the ith district}}$ |
| 3. | Decadal district rural to rural in-migration rate. | DMRR | $\frac{\text{Decadal rural to rural male in-migrants of the ith district}}{\text{Total rural male population of the ith district}}$ |
| 4. | Decadal district rural to urban in-migration rate | DMRU | $\frac{\text{Decadal rural to urban in-migrants of the ith district}}{\text{Total urban male population of the ith district}}$ |
| 5. | Decadal Net Inter-district migration rate | NIDM | $\frac{\text{In-out (male) migrants of the ith district}}{\text{Male population of the ith district}}$ |
| 6. | | PDM | Pooled data for 1971 and 1981 for decadal district in-migration |
| 7. | | PDMR | Pooled data for 1971 and 1981 for decadal district in-migration excluding intra-district in-migration. |
| 8. | | PDMRR | Pooled data for 1971 and 1981 for decadal rural to rural district in-migration. |
| 9. | | PDMRU | Pooled data for 1971 and 1981 for decadal rural to urban district in-migration. |
| 10. | | PNIDM | Pooled data for net inter-district migration. |

## 6.2 HYPOTHESES

The hypotheses underlying the models are as follows[1].

1. In-migration is high where the *degree of Urbanization* is high and out-migration, from the low degree of urbanization. Degree of urbanization is probably a proxy for the availability of wide range of occupations. It is also likely to be proxy for some of the psychic benefits, in that cities may be more interesting to live in than rural areas. Consequently, both retention and expulsion forces operate and a prior sign is not predicted for the variable (Mehta, B.C. 1975, 1978; Mohan Rakesh, 1985; Bawa, K.S. and G.S. Kainth, 1985).
2. In-migration is high where the water supply is assured. The normal rainfall is taken as proxy for assured water supply. Scanty of and uncertainty of water are the push and plenty of and certainty of water are pull factors (Mehta, B.C., 1975; 1978). But in places of uncertainty of water, some special industries may develop, which may act as retention or attraction force. So the relationship is unpredictable.
3. The political and administrative factors have a considerable impact on the level of migration. The pattern of government expenditure in favour of *centres of administration* acts as a pull force. Because biased governmental expenditure may result into benefits (Preston, S.H.).
4. *Density of population* is expected to influence migration. Higher density of population may be the result of urbanization. So it may act as a pull

---

1. For reviews of the literature from which the expected signs are derived see (B.C. Mehta; 1978, J. King; 1970, K.S. Bawa; 1985; G.S. Kainth; 1985).

force due to initial economies of scale. But if it results in overcrowding, then diseconomies may begin to operate. In such a case, it will act as a push force. So the relationship is open-ended (Zipf, 1946; Fabricant, 1970; Greenwood, 1970; Dandekar, 1974).

5. District with higher availability of *agricultural output* results in surplus of output. So the people migrating from outside must be certain of it and the factor works as a pull force.
6. Higher the percentage of *social backwardness,* lesser will be in and out migration. Thus retention and expulsion forces operate in opposite directions and *a priori* sign attached to the coefficient is to be negative (Schultz, 1971; Mehta, B.C. 1975, 1978).
7. *Transport* is likely to be a proxy for the cost of moving. Migration will take place when the benefits of migration are perceived to exceed the cost of moving. (Amrit, 1966; Agarwal, 1958). As the value of this variable rises, the rate of in and out migration should rise and a positive sign is expected to the coefficient of the variable.
8. *Distance* is generally regarded as a proxy for some of the costs of moving and for the information available about the contemplated area. The greater the distance involved, the greater will be the direct costs of moving and of return visits to friends and relatives. The retention force operates to reduce out-migration while at the same a repulsion force reduces in-migration. A negative sign is expected to the coefficient of the variable (Mehta, B.C. 1975, 1978; Sahota, 1968, Schuwartz, 1973).
9. *The migrant stock* variable has been regarded as a proxy for some of the direct and opportunity costs of migration that are implied by the prospect of living in new area and searching for employment.

These may be lowered significantly if there are friends and relatives from one's area of origin that can provide material support and aid in obtaining employment. It may also be a proxy for the psychic costs of moving and adjustment, these may be lower if friends and relatives are present.

This variable represents the stock of migrants in the past. Hence, these past forces via this variable affect current migration, perhaps in terms of the formation of expectations. The greater is the past migration to an area, the more likely a favourable opinion of that area is held by the prospective migrants. Thus it may be said that forces of attraction and expulsion are at work. The destination area becomes more attractive as the migrant stock increases and it becomes easier to leave the area of origin. In consequence, *a priori* positive sign is attached to the coefficient of this variable (Greenwood, M. 1969; Gupta, S. 1967; King, J. 1970).

10. *Average age of the population* reflects the expected duration of a migrant acting as a potential investor. The younger a person, the more the time to recoup an investment. Thus the younger the community is on the average, the higher would be the probability of out-migration. So with this repulsion force, a positive sign to the coefficient of this variable is attached (King, J. 1970; Dandekar, 1974).
11. *Education* is likely to be a proxy for the ability to migrate. Assuming that educated or literate persons are more efficient in their activities. Education is associated with a lower cost of migration and increase in the flow of information, concerning new areas, thus lowering the risk of migration. Moreover, if the destination place is having total number of educational institutions more than the

origin place, then pull and push forces both operate in the same direction. And *a priori* positive sign is attached to the coefficient of the variable (Sabot, 1975; Schultz, 1975; Lipton, 1976).

12. If in the destination place the number of *banks and credit facilities* are more than the source area, then the migrants will have more opportunity to develop in their occupation. So pull and push forces work in the same direction; a positive sign is assumed for the coefficient of the variable (Stouffer, 1946).
13. Agricultural labourers are the landless labourers and very small farmers whose main source of income, in view of small holdings, is wage employment. Their condition is miserable. They do not get work on regular basis and they are severely exploited by land-owners with the increase in proletarisation of land they are coming towards urban areas to get employment. Moreover with the increased mechanization in agriculture, they are being evacuated from their origin place. In this case, positive sign is expected for rural to urban migration. But sign is unpredictable for rural to rural in-migration. No *priori* sign is given to the coefficient of the variable.
14. *Livestock* is an important source of income. Livestock products like meat, milk and milk products have a prominent place in the dietary habits of people in the advanced countries. In fact, pastoral production is far more resilient than crop production and more remunerative too (Sundharam; 1985). Livestock works as a subsidiary occupation for income generation particularly in the semi-arid and arid

---

Null hypotheses ($H_0$) in all cases is that the variable does not influence migration. Signs given here refer to the alternative hypotheses.

areas. The role of the variable in influencing migration is unpredictable. It depends on whether with the increase in income people want to diversify their jobs or not (King, 1980).

15. *Industrial development* is a proxy for the probability of an individual in destination area, finding a job in that area in a given period of time and given expenditures on search. As the value of this variable rises, the pull and push forces operate in the same direction, therefore, a positive sign is assigned to the coefficient (Mehta, 1975, 1978).
16. *Medical facilities* serve as pull force for the process of migration. As the quantum of migration depends upon the opportunities and facilities at the place of destination relative to the place of origin and also relative to all other alternatives available, the prospective migrants, the expected sign of the coefficient of the variable is to be positive (Stouffer, 1946; Mehta, 1975, 1978).
17. If *mechanization of agriculture* is in operation, then the farmers will have more chances to earn more income. The retention force will work but at the same time, with the increase in income, they will be diversifying their jobs. They may migrate to other places. The sign of the coefficient is indeterminate a *priori.*
18. If the *prospects of development* of an area are brighter, the migrants will be having indication of more jobs, higher income and better standard of living. Pull force would work, therefore, positive sign may be attached to the coefficient of the variable.

Thus, the forces affecting migration are broken down into pull forces and push forces. These are further sub-divided, pull forces may be either retention or attraction forces. If a retention force is operating, an increase in the value of a given independent variable is seen as increasing the attractiveness or benefits associated with a given area, thus decreasing the out-migration rate. If an attraction force is operating, it is the in-migration rate that increases. Push forces may be either expulsion or repulsion forces. If an expulsion force is operating, an increase in the value of a given independent variable decreases the desirability of residence in a given area, thus inducing a rise in the out-migrating rate. If a repulsion force is operating, it is the in-migration rate that falls.

A regression equation using the migration rate as the dependent variable and other aggregate rates as independent variables explains the behaviour of a group of people, but not directly the behaviour of individuals. However, the migration rate may be interpreted as the probability of an individual migrating, that is, if the migration rate rises, the more likely it is that a randomly selected individual will belong to the group of migrants.

In this study, model is built to explain inter-regional differences in migration. The variables indicating these differences may be of three types —

(i) Policy variables which can be controlled and directed;
(ii) Non-policy exogenous variables;
(iii) Endogenous variables.

The presence of endogenous variable as an explanatory variable in the model may cause double way causation and create the problem of simultaneity bias. The problem is not likely to arise in the present exercise because, in base year, lagged values of explanatory variables are taken.[1]

---

1. Mehta & Mehta (1991) have developed the Demographic Economic Interaction Model and found that the system turns out to be recursive and O.L.S. provides unbiased estimates.

## 6.3 RESULTS

This Section is further divided into sub-sections to deal with the different dependent variables while the set of independent variables remaining the same.

### 6.3A Decadal District in-migration model (DM), 1971-1981

This model includes male decadal in-migration in the district from short, medium and long distance i.e. intra-district, inter-district and inter-state in-migration in the district is combined.

Table 6.2 shows the hypothesized signs, estimated correlation coefficients between dependent variable (DM) and the various explanatory variables and summarizes the subsequent discussion of the theoretical relevance of each variable in the decadal district in-migration model.

**TABLE 6.2**

**Hypothesised Signs and Estimated Correlation Coefficients for the Decadal District In-Migration (Males) Model (DM), 1971, 1981**

| *S.No.* | *Explanatory variables* | *Hypothesized Signs* | *Estimated correlation coefficient with DM* | |
|---|---|---|---|---|
| | | | *1971* | *1981* |
| 1 | 2 | 3 | 4 | 5 |
| 1. | DP | ? | - 0.17 | - 0.28 |
| 2. | SB | ? | 0.30 | 0.14 |
| 3. | CA | + | 0.02 | 0.50* |
| 4. | DU | ? | 0.16 | 0.03 |
| 5. | PD | + | 0.48* | 0.50* |
| 6. | D | - | - 0.42* | - 0.52* |
| 7. | ED | + | 0.09 | 0.04 |
| 8. | TP | + | 0.02 | 0.06 |
| 9. | ID | + | 0.34* | 0.43* |
| 10. | MF | + | 0.13 | 0.05 |

*(cont.)*

| 1 | 2 | 3 | 4 | 5 |
|---|---|---|---|---|
| 11. | WR | ? | 0.02 | 0.09 |
| 12. | MECA | ? | 0.44* | 0.78* |
| 13. | AGO | + | 0.10 | 0.26 |
| 14. | BAC | + | 0.09 | 0.38* |
| 15. | SMR | + | 0.74* | 0.91* |
| 16. | AA | + | 0.02 | 0.15 |
| 17. | LIV | ? | 0.02 | 0.05 |
| 18. | AL | ? | 0.07 | 0.20 |
| | N | | 26 | 26 |

Critical value: (1 Tail; .05) = + or - (.33)
(2 Tail; .05) = +/- (.39)
*Significant at 5% level of significance
Note: Sign? implies open-ended hypothesis.

On the basis of the hypotheses developed in the preceding Section, it is postulated that Social Backwardness (SB) and Distance (D) are negatively related with decadal district in-migration whereas the other variable Centres of Administration (CA), Prospective Development (PD), Education Development (ED), Transport Facilities (TP), Industrial Development (ID), Medical Facilities (MF), Agricultural Output (AGO), Banking and Credit (BAC), Stock of Migrants (SMR) and Average Age (AA) of the population are positively related.

Table 6.2 reveals that only some of the correlation coefficients of the dependent variable with independent variables are high and significant at 5 per cent level of significance. The variable SB is not having expected sign in both the census periods in 1971 and 1981. The wrong sign may be due to the interaction of the explanatory forces in the model.

In Table 6.3, regression results are satisfactory. In equation 6.3.1, more than 90 per cent variation in the dependent variable, decadal district (male) in-migration (DM) is explained by the explanatory variables Social Backwardness (SB), Prospective Development (PD), Transport Facilities (TP), Industrial

Development (ID), Agricultural Output (AGO), Banking and Credit (BAC), Stock of Migrants (SMR) and Average Age (AA) of the population. In equation 6.3.2, more than 94 per cent variation in the dependent variable is explained by the variables Degree of Urbanisation (DU), Prospective Development (PD), Industrial Development (ID), Water Resources (WR), and Agriculture Labour (AL). In both the equations, common variables are: PD, ID, SMR. In equation 6.3.2, the variable PD is significant at 5 per cent level while in equation 6.3.1 it was at 1 per cent level. ID and SMR retained their level of significance.

**TABLE 6.3**

**Coefficients and "t" Values obtained in Estimating Regression Equations for Decadal District In-Migration (Male) Model (DM), 1971, 1981**

| *S. No.* | *Equation No. Variable Exp / Dep* | *6.3.1.* *DM 1971* | *6.3.2.* *DM 1981* | *6.3.3* *DM-SMR 1971* | *6.3.4.* *DM-SMR 1981* | *6.3.5* *DM 1971+1981* |
|---|---|---|---|---|---|---|
| 1 | 2 | 3 | 4 | 5 | 6 | 7 |
| 1. | DP | — | — | — | -0.0116* (1.71) | -0.0002 (2.57) |
| 2. | SB | 0.0020* (4.62) | — | 0.0016** (2.18) | — | 0.0012* (3.56) |
| 3. | CA | — | — | — | — | — |
| 4. | DU | — | -0.0012* (-4.84) | -0.0062* (-2.95) | — | — |
| 5. | PD | 0.0011* (3.62) | 0.0002** (1.75) | 0.0016* (3.26) | 0.0006** (2.33) | 0.0004** (1.70) |
| 6. | D | — | — | — | — | 0.0003** (1.93) |
| 7. | ED | — | — | 0.0263 (1.01) | 0.0341* (2.76) | — |

*(cont.)*

| 1 | 2 | 3 | 4 | 5 | 6 | 7 |
|---|---|---|---|---|---|---|
| 8. | TP | 0.0414** (2.31) | — | .0746* (2.78) | — | — |
| 9. | ID | 0.0085** (2.22) | 0.0048** (2.38) | 0.0164** (2.37) | 0.0178* (5.54) | 0.0119* (4.45) |
| 10. | MF | — | — | 0.0014** (2.00) | — | — |
| 11. | WR | — | -0.0085*** (-1.94) | — | — | — |
| 12. | MECA | — | — | 0.0214* (5.02) | — | — |
| 13. | AGO | 0.0074 (1.07) | — | — | 0.0380* (8.32) | 0.0099** (1.72) |
| 14. | BAC | 0.0257** (2.89) | — | 0.0450* (2.51) | — | — |
| 15. | SMR | 0.1414 (8.57) | 0.8251* (12.79) | — | — | 0.1216* (5.26) |
| 16. | AA | -0.0024 (1.08) | — | — | — | — |
| 17. | LIV | — | — | — | 0.0004** (2.72) | — |
| 18. | AL | — | 0.0018 (1.09) | — | — | — |
| 19. | DVT | — | — | — | — | — |
| | Constant | 0.0095 | 0.0362 | -0.0262 | 0.0758 | 0.0318 |
| | $R^2$ | 0.9061* | 0.9410* | 0.8035* | 0.8923* | 0.7587 |
| | $\overline{R}^2$ | 0.8619 | 0.9223 | 0.6930 | 0.8582 | 0.7203 |
| | F value | 20.51 | 50.460 | 7.269 | 26.223 | 19.762 |
| | n | 26 | 26 | 26 | 26 | 52 |

The figures in parantheses below the regression coefficients are the respective "t" ratios.

* Significant at 1% level of significance.

** Significant at 5% level of significance.

*** Significant at 10% level of significance.

While looking at results of equations 6.3.1 and 6.3.2, it is found that the variable SMR is having large "t" value, its "t" value is greater than the "t" values of other variables. Moreover, when the elasticity of regression coefficient at the mean value is calculated, SMR appears to be most important variable. To find out the extent to which this variable (SMR) contributes to $R^2$ of both the equations, it is dropped from 6.3.1 and 6.3.2 and regression is re-run. These results are given in equations 6.3.3 and 6.3.4. Again the results are satisfactory, more than 80 per cent variation in the district in-migration is explained by the equation 6.3.3 and variables responsible for this variation are SB, DU, PD, TP, ID, MF, WR, MECA, BAC. Almost all the variables have come upto the expectations. In equation 6.3.4, a little better results are obtained. More than 90 per cent variation in the dependent variables is explained by DP, PD, ED, ID, AGO, LIV. And all the variables exhibit the expected signs.

While comparing the results of 6.3.1 and 6.3.3 for 1971, a change in the level of significance for some of the variables is noted. The level of significance of TP and BAC is increased from 5 per cent to 1 per cent, of SB it is reduced from 1 per cent to 5 per cent, whereas PD and ID are on the same level of significance.

While comparing equations 6.3.3 with 6.3.4 for 1981., it is found that the common entered variables are PD and ID. The level of significance for ID rises from 5 per cent to 1 per cent and of PD remains same at 5 per cent.

$R^2$ of all the models is significant at 1 per cent level of significance, which shows the fit is good. The results point out that in-migration of the male population increases with prospective development and other facilities available in the destination district. The previous migrants from the same origin place also play important role in migratory movement. Moreover, younger population is more prone to migration.

In case of SMR variable, when it is dropped from the equation, the signs and magnitudes of regression coefficients are not changed substantially, so it is not a dominant variable.* It is an important and significant variable to influence in-migration of districts.**

For the structural change, if any, in the two census periods, 1971 and 1981, data are pooled with the same set of explanatory variables and the estimated results are given in 6.3.5. In the estimation of this equation, "Time" dummy variable, DVT, is statistically not significant. The "t" ratio is much less than 1. Hence, it does not enter into the step by step regression analysis. It supports the hypothesis that there is no significant structural change in the decadal district in-migration pattern of males between the two census periods, *1971* and *1981*.

### 6.3B. Decadal District In-migration (Male) Model Excluding Intra-District in Migration (DME) 1971, 1981

Distance is a "traditional proxy for migration costs—psychic, pecuniary and opportunity" (Schultz). It is negatively correlated with migration. Short distance (intra-district) in-migration dominates the migration stream. It has also been shown, it is predominantly for demographic reasons of marriage and birth. Hence, it may be desirable to concentrate on migration stream than intra-district migration.

The estimated correlation coefficients between the dependent variable and the explanatory variables are given in Table 6.4.

---

* The presence of dominant variable may change the sign of the coefficients of other variables. (Raw & Miller; 1975, 43).

** Greenwood (1969, 1970), Vedder and Gallaway (1972), Levy & Wadycki (1973) and Jonathan King (1970) among others have included "Migrant Stock" variable in their explanatory models. In general, these authors have obtained positive and highly statistically significant coefficient on the "Migrant Stock". The proper interpretation of these results and of the migrant stock variable, however, is not a settled.matter.

**TABLE 6.4**

**Hypothesized Signs and Estimated Correlation Co-efficients for the Decadal District In-Migration (Male) Model Excluding Intra-District In-Migration (Male) (DME)—1971, 1981**

| *S.No.* | *Explanatory variables* | *Hypothesized Signs* | *Estimated correlation coefficients with DME* | |
|---|---|---|---|---|
| | | | *1971* | *1981* |
| 1. | DP | ? | 0.01 | - 0.43* |
| 2. | SB | - | 0.17 | 0.24 |
| 3. | CA | + | - 0.11 | 0.41* |
| 4. | DU | ? | - 0.25 | - 0.05 |
| 5. | PD | + | 0.13 | 0.53* |
| 6. | D | - | - 0.18 | - 0.50* |
| 7. | ED | + | 0.26 | - 0.13 |
| 8. | TP | + | 0.25 | 0.14 |
| 9. | ID | + | 0.08 | 0.21 |
| 10. | MF | + | 0.09 | 0.01 |
| 11. | WR | ? | 0.02 | 0.15 |
| 12. | MECA | ? | 0.13 | 0.76* |
| 13. | AGO | + | 0.19 | 0.31 |
| 14. | BAC | + | 0.21 | 0.22 |
| 15. | SMR | + | 0.40* | 0.88* |
| 16. | AA | + | 0.20 | 0.07 |
| 17. | LIV | ? | 0.31 | 0.09 |
| 18. | AL | ? | -0.13 | 0.11 |
| | N | | 26 | 26 |

Critical value : (1 Tail; .05) = + or - (.33)
(2 Tail; .05) = +/- (.39)

* Significant at 5% level of significance

Note: Sign? refers to open-ended hypothesis.

Table 6.4 reveals that only some of the correlation coefficients are having signs opposite to the hypothesized signs, whereas the correlation coefficients of some are significant at 5 per cent level of significance. The highest correlation in the Table is shown by the variable SMR in both the census periods 1971 and 1981.

The stepwise regression results of the model are given in Table 6.5.

**TABLE 6.5**

**Coefficients and "t" Values Obtained in Estimating Regression Equations for Decadal District In-Migration Excluding Intra-District (Male) In-Migration, 1971, 1981**

| *S.No.* | *Equation No. Variables Dep Exp* | *6.5.1 DME'71* | *6.5.2 DME'81* | *6.5.3 DME 71+81* |
|---|---|---|---|---|
| 1. | DP | — | - .0008* (-4.10) | — |
| 2. | SB | - .0069* (-6.08) | — | 0.0026** (1.99) |
| 3. | CA | — | .0102 (1.15) | — |
| 4. | DU | — | — | — |
| 5. | PD | — | — | — |
| 6. | D | — | — | - 0.0005 (-1.27) |
| 7. | ED | — | 0.0817* (3.32) | — |
| 8. | TP | — | — | — |
| 9. | ID | — | — | 0.0163** (1.896) |
| 10. | MF | — | — | — |
| 11. | WR | — | — | — |
| 12. | MECA | — | .0116*** (1.54) | — |

*(cont.)*

| S.No. | *Equation No.* *Variables Dep* *Exp* | *6.5.1* *DME'71* | *6.5.2* *DME'81* | *6.5.3* *DME 71+81* |
|---|---|---|---|---|
| 13. | AGO | — | — | — |
| 14. | BAC | — | — | -- |
| 15. | SMR | — | — | — |
| 16. | AA | — | — | — |
| 17. | LIV | .0027* (4.62) | .0008* (3.34) | 0.0006 (1.03) |
| 18. | AL | - .0191*** (2.10) | - .0043 (1.18) | — |
| 19. | DVT | — | — | — |
| | Constant | - .0558 | - .0437 | - 0.0314 |
| | $R^2$ | .2809** | .7229* | 0.1491** |
| | $\overline{R}^2$ | .1828 | .6446 | 0.0767 |
| | F Value | 2.865 | 8.558 | 2.059 |
| | n | 26 | 26 | 52 |

Values in parantheses below the regression coefficients are the respective "t" ratios.

* 1% level of significance.

** 5% level of significance.

*** 10% level of significance.

In the Table 6.5, equation 6.5.1 for decadal district in-migration (male) excluding intra-district in-migration (male) explains only 28 per cent variation in the dependent variable DME, 1971. The signs of the parameter estimates of three variables social backwardness (SB), development of livestock (LIV) and agriculture labour (AL) tally with hypothesized signs.

Equation 6.5.2 for 1981 explains 72 per cent of the total variation in the dependent variable DME, 1981. The estimated signs of the coefficients of the variables : Density of Population (DP), Centres of Administration (CA), Education Development

(ED), Mechanization in Agriculture (MECA), Development of Livestock (LIV) and Agriculture Labour (AL) are in accordance with the expected signs. In estimation of equation 6.5.1 (1971) and 6.5.2 (1981), only two variables LIV and AL are common. The level of significance of LIV remains same in the two equations, whereas AL loses the significance in 1981. The overall fit for 1981 is better than 1971. These results point out that developed centres having facilities are likely to attract more in-migrants. The variable LIV positively influences migration. With the increase in income due to development of livestock (LIV), people migrate to the developed area to diversify their jobs or to improve their standard of living.

In the pooled data equation 6.5.3, temporal dummy variable DVT does not enter and only 15 per cent variation in the dependent variable is explained. Since the coefficient of dummy variable (DVT) is found to be not significant at 5 per cent level of significance, there is no structural shift between 1971 and 1981. However, since the different variables enter in the regression equations for 1971, 1981 and for pooled data, structural change in migration stream is evidenced.

### 6.3C. Rural to Rural Decadal District (Male) In-migration Model (DMRR, 1971, 1981)

In the four streams of inmigration, R-R, R-U, U-R and U-U, R-R occupies a dominant position* because most of the rural people migrate to other rural places due to availability of resources for their farming and other facilities.

The Table 6.6 shows the hypothesized signs and estimated correlation coefficients for the rural-rural district (male) in-migration for the census period 1971 and 1981[1]. A few of the

---

* M.K. Premi (1983) observed, R-R migration has declined but it would remain a dominant stream in Indian migration for several decades, particularly till the end of the present century.

1. Total district decadal district rural to rural in-migration (including intra-district).

variables are having opposite signs. In 1971, no variable is significantly correlated, whereas in 1981 some of them are significantly correlated.

**TABLE 6.6**

**Hypothesized Signs and Estimated Correlation Coefficients for the Rural to Rural Decadal District (Male) In-Migration Model (DMRR), 1971, 1981**

| *S.No.* | *Explanatory variables* | *Hypothesized Signs* | *Estimated correlation coefficients with DMRR* | |
|---|---|---|---|---|
| | | | *1971* | *1981* |
| 1. | DP | ? | - 0.01 | - 0.21 |
| 2. | SB | - | 0.28 | 0.06 |
| 3. | CA | + | 0.01 | 0.59* |
| 4. | DU | ? | - 0.01 | - 0.02 |
| 5. | PD | + | 0.07 | 0.47* |
| 6. | D | - | - 0.04 | - 0.37* |
| 7. | ED | + | 0.07 | 0.27 |
| 8. | TP | + | 0.14 | 0.07 |
| 9. | ID | + | 0.20 | 0.39* |
| 10. | MF | + | - 0.08 | 0.16 |
| 11. | WR | ? | 0.03 | - 0.08 |
| 12. | MECA | ? | 0.06 | - 0.47* |
| 13. | AGO | + | 0.03 | 0.20 |
| 14. | BAC | + | 0.05 | 0.26 |
| 15. | SMR | + | 0.18 | 0.54* |
| 16. | AA | + | 0.01 | 0.15 |
| 17. | LIV | ? | - 0.17 | 0.26 |
| 18. | AL | ? | 0.22 | 0.02 |
| | N | | 26 | 26 |

Critical value: (1 Tail; .05) = + or - (.33)
(2 Tail; .05) = +/- (.39)

*Significant at 5% level of significance

Note: Sign? implies open-ended hypothesis.

The subsequent regression estimates are given in Table 6.7.

**TABLE 6.7**

**Coefficients and "t" Values Obtained in Estimating Regression Equations for Rural to Rural Decadal District In-Migration (Male) Model, DMRR 1971, 1981**

| *S.No.* | *Equation No. Variables Dep Exp* | *6.7.1 (DMR) 1971* | *6.7.2 (DMR) 1981* | *6.7.3 (DMR-SMR) 1981* | *6.7.4 (DMR) (1971+1981)* |
|---|---|---|---|---|---|
| 1. | DP | 0.0014* (3.538) | — | - 0.0002* (-3.77) | — |
| 2. | SB | — | — | — | — |
| 3. | CA | — | — | — | 0.0071** (2.20) |
| 4. | DU | — | — | — | — |
| 5. | PD | 0.0018* (2.732) | 0.004* (3.175) | — | — |
| 6. | D | — | - 0.002*** (-1.465) | - 0.0002*** (1.35) | — |
| 7. | ED | 0.1609* (4.159) | — | — | 0.0167* (3.24) |
| 8. | TP | — | — | 0.0006** (2.13) | — |
| 9. | ID | — | - 0.0025*** (1.459) | — | — |
| 10. | MF | — | — | — | — |
| 11. | WR | — | 0.0035 (1.039) | 0.0077 (1.48) | — |
| 12. | MECA | — | — | 0.0267* (5.20) | — |
| 13. | AGO | 0.0154 (1.085) | — | 0.0186* (2.84) | 0.0087*** (1.64) |

*(cont.)*

| S.No. | Equation No. Variables Dep Exp | 6.7.1 (DMR) 1971 | 6.7.2 (DMR) 1981 | 6.7.3 (DMR-SMR) 1981 | 6.7.4 (DMR) (1971+1981) |
|---|---|---|---|---|---|
| 14. | BAC | — | — | 0.0306* (3.26) | — |
| 15. | SMR | 0.1359* (3.505) | 0.7277* (13.621) | — | 0.0319* (4.21) |
| 16. | AA | 0.0056 (1.302) | 0.0017*** (1.496) | 0.0030*** (1.75) | — |
| 17. | LIV | — | — | 0.0418* (4.35) | 0.0003 (1.50) |
| 18. | AL | - 0.0114*** (-1.901) | — | — | — |
| 19. | DVT | | | | 0.0520* (3.12) |
| | Constant | 0.0905 | 0.0650 | 0.0418 | 0.1206 |
| | $R^2$ | 0.6117* | 0.9480* | 0.9171* | 0.4311* |
| | $\overline{R}^2$ | 0.4607 | 0.9278 | 0.8618 | 0.3553 |
| | F ratio | 4.051 | 46.909 | 16.593 | 5.684 |
| | N | 26 | 26 | 26 | 52 |

The figures in parantheses below the regression coefficients are respective "t" values.

* 1% level of significance.

** 5% level of significance.

*** 10% level of significance.

The equation 6.7.1 of Table 6.7 for DMRR 1971 explains the 61 per cent variation in the dependent variable rural to rural decadal district in-migration (male). The coefficients of the included explanatory variables, density of population (DP), prospective development (PD), education development (ED), agricultural output (AGO), stock of migrants (SMR), average age of the population (AA) and agriculture labour (AL) exhibit the hypothesized effects.

The equation 6.7.2 for DMR 1981 explains the 94 per cent variation in the dependent variable. The coefficients of the explanatory variables prospective development (PD), distance (D), industrial development (ID), water resources (WR), stock of migrants (SMR) and average age (AA) of the population have come up to the expected sign except the sign of the coefficient of the variable industrial development (ID) opposite sign of the parameter estimate of the variable may be due to the nature of this model. It is the rural to rural in-migration model and industrial development is not important. Rural migration is mainly due to the relative transformation of agriculture or other facilities available for farming in the destination region. Even in this model, the role of prior migrants (SMR) to attract new migrants is important.

High regression coefficient and "t" value of SMR is noted. Moreover, while calculating elasticity of the regression coefficient at the mean value, SMR seems to be most important variable.

To observe the extent to which it has influenced the dependent variable DMRR or whether it is a dominant variable, equation 6.7.2 is re-estimated with SMR excluded. It is clear from the Table 6.7 that the explanatory power of the model is reduced by 3-4 per cent. However, while looking at the common included variables in 6.7.2 and 6.7.3 (WR, DI and AA), there is no change in the signs and levels of the significance of the parameter values in the two regressions. It can be said that SMR is an important variable in influencing rural to rural in-migration of the districts.

While comparing the results of 6.7.1 with 6.7.2 (of 1971 and 1981) only three variables (PD, SMR and AA) are common. PD and SMR have same level of significance in 1971 and 1981, whereas the variable AA becomes insignificant in 1981. The explanatory power of the 1981 model is more than 1971.

To have a glance at the structural change in the two periods under consideration, a regression is re-run for the pooled data in equation 6.7.4. The temporal dummy variable DVT enters in the estimation of the equation and it is significant at 1 per cent level of significance. So there is evidence of a structural change in the rural to rural in-migration of districts in 1981 in comparison to the year 1971.

### 6.3D Rural to Urban Decadal District In-Migration (Male) Model (DMRU) 1971, 1981

Rural to urban in-migration is next to rural to rural in-migration. It is also sizeable.[1] The rural people migrate to urban areas to diversify their jobs, to increase the education for their children or for other amenities available in urban areas. The greater the difference in economic opportunities between rural and urban areas, the greater the flow of migrants will be from rural to urban areas. The decision to migrate depends on urban-rural wage differential (Todaro).

Table 6.8 reveals estimated correlation coefficients between dependent variables, decadal rural to urban in-migration of the district and other explanatory variables in 1971 and 1981.

The variables, degree of urbanization, prospective development of the districts, medical facilities are highly correlated with rural to urban in-migration of males. These relationships conform generally accepted view that difference in rural and urban areas with regard to economic infrastructural development are main reasons for migration.[2]

---

1. M.K. Premi (1983).
2. Including intra-district rural to urban in-migration (male).

**TABLE 6.8**

**Hypothesized Signs and Estimated Correlation Coefficients for the Rural to Urban Decadal District (Male) In-Migration Model (DMRU), 1971, 1981**

| *S.No.* | *Explanatory variables* | *Hypothesized Signs* | *Estimated correlation coefficient with DMRU* | |
|---|---|---|---|---|
| | | | *1971* | *1981* |
| 1. | DP | ? | - 0.19 | - 0.19 |
| 2. | SB | - | - 0.24 | - 0.17 |
| 3. | CA | + | + 0.47* | + 0.43* |
| 4. | DU | ? | 0.45* | + 0.25* |
| 5. | PD | + | + 0.62* | + 0.55* |
| 6. | D | - | - 0.37* | - 0.37* |
| 7. | ED | + | + 0.35* | + 0.22 |
| 8. | TP | + | + 0.33 | + 0.15 |
| 9. | ID | + | + 0.60* | + 0.64* |
| 10. | MF | + | + 0.73* | + 0.37* |
| 11. | WR | ? | + 0.10 | + 0.19 |
| 12. | MECA | ? | + 0.19 | + 0.29 |
| 13. | AGO | + | + 0.27 | + 0.17 |
| 14. | BAC | + | + 0.23 | + 0.56* |
| 15. | SMR | + | + 0.22 | + 0.46* |
| 16. | AA | + | + 0.41* | + 0.51* |
| 17. | LIV | ? | - 0.19 | + 0.01 |
| 18. | AL | ? | + 0.24 | + 0.44* |
| | n | | 26 | 26 |

Critical value : (1 Tail; .05) = + or - (.33)
(2 Tail; .05) = +/- (.39)
* Significant at 5% level of significance

Note: The sign ? refers to open—ended relationship.

The results of the estimated regression equation are given in following Table 6.9

**TABLE 6.9**

**Coefficients and "t" Value Obtained in Estimating Regression Equations for Rural to Urban (Male) In-Migration DMRU, 1971, 1981**

| *S. No.* | *Equation No. Variables Dep Exp* | *6.9.1 DMRU 1971* | *6.9.2 DMRU 1981* | *6.9.3 DMRU 1971+1981* |
|---|---|---|---|---|
| 1 | 2 | 3 | 4 | 5 |
| 1. | DP | + 0.0001** (1.78) | — | — |
| 2. | SB | + 0.0002 (1.06) | — | — |
| 3. | CA | — | + 0.0064** (2.21) | + 0.0026 (1.26) |
| 4. | DU | + 0.0017* (9.37) | — | — |
| 5. | PD | — | + 0.0006* (4.99) | — |
| 6. | D | - 0.0002* (-7.50) | — | - 0.0001* (3.33) |
| 7. | ED | — | — | — |
| 8. | TP | — | — | + 0.0003* (8.72) |
| 9. | ID | + 0.0047* (5.33) | + 0.0115* (7.35) | + 0.0083* (8.72) |
| 10. | MF | — | — | + 0.0004* (4.34) |
| 11. | WR | - 0.0007 (-1.16) | — | — |
| 12. | MECA | — | — | 0.0018** (2.18) |
| 13. | AGO | + 0.0026*** (1.40) | + 0.0084* (2.81) | - 0.0025 (-1.12) |
| 14. | BAC | + 0.0105* (3.85) | — | — |

*(cont.)*

| 1 | 2 | 3 | 4 | 5 |
|---|---|---|---|---|
| 15. | SMR | — | + 0.0655 (1.37) | — |
| 16. | AA | 0.0005 (1.28) | — | + 0.0015* (2.89) |
| 17. | LIV | - | - | — |
| 18. | AL | 0.0009 (1.50) | + 0.0053* (4.42) | — |
| 19. | DVT | | | 0.0100** (2.98) |
| | Constant | - 0.553 | - 0.0096 | 0.0473 |
| | $R^2$ | 0.9640* | 0.8856* | 0.8614* |
| | $\overline{R}^2$ | 0.9400 | 0.8495 | 0.8317 |
| | F ratio | 40.135 | 24.516 | 29.003 |
| | N | 26 | 26 | 52 |

The figures in brackets below the regression coefficients are respective "t" values.

* 1% level of significance.

** 5% level of significance.

*** 10% level of significance.

The equation 6.9.1 for 1971 reveals, the signs of estimated regression coefficients of all the variables except Social Backwardness (SB) are in accordance with hypotheses. In rural to urban in-migration in 1971, the Industrial Development (ID) and Banking and Credit (BAC) are the important variables. Industrial Development (ID) is highly statistically significant in both the years 1971 and 1981, whereas BAC and ID create job opportunities and have positive effect on district rural-urban in-migration[1] the significant variable Distance (D) points out that distance hampers rural to urban migration.

1. Ranjana Jain (1991) in her Ph.D. thesis "Urbanization in India" has also found industrialisation is a strong, positive and statistically significant stable determinant of urbanization. Infrastructural development and number of capital towns are other important variables found in her study.

Equation 6.9.2 for 1981 shows that important variables are Prospective Development of the districts (PD), Industrial Development (ID), Agricultural Output (AGO) and Agricultural Labour (AL). PD and ID increase the job opportunities and AGO is related with the increase in income of the rural people. With the increase in this income, they want to diversify their jobs and rural to urban in-migration increases. Rural proletarisation (AL) leads to increase in urbanward migration.

The common variables in 1971 and 1981 are ID, AGO and AL. Whereas ID retains the same level of significance in 1981 as 1971, for AGO it rises from 10 per cent to 1 per cent in 1981 and AL becomes significant at 1 per cent level of significance in 1981. The variation explained by equation 6.9.1 (1971) is 96 per cent of the total variation in dependent variable. This explanatory power is reduced in 1981. The equation 6.9.2 (1981) explains 88 per cent variation in the dependent variable.

Temporal dummy variable (DVT) for the pooled data 1971 and 1981 is significant at 1 per cent level of significance. so there is structural shift in rural to urban in-migration in 26 districts of Rajasthan. Different set of explanatory variables is included in the analysis of separately for 1971 and 1981 and even for the pooled data of 1971 and 1981. The regression results point out that the trend of rural people to migrate to urban areas still continues and this remain till the disparity in the rural and urban sector prevails in the economy.

While comparing decadal district rural to rural in-migration (male) and rural to urban in-migration (male), the regression results points out that ruralward migration is due to relative development of destination rural areas and urbanward migration is due to the facilities and amenities available in urban areas in comparison to rural areas.

### 6.3E Decadal Net Inter-district (Male) In-Migration Model NIDM, 1871, 1981

This sub-section is related to medium distance in-migration i.e. in-migration between districts in Rajasthan. Before 1971 census, it was not possible to built inter-district migration model.[1] In this model, dummy variable (DV) is introduced. In Rajasthan, out of the 26 districts, 17 districts are having contiguous borders with other states and their inter-district migration is negligible. To classify such districts DV=0 stands for border districts and in other case DV=1. The null hypothesis is that there is no difference in the pattern of migration of border and non-border districts. Whereas the alternative hypotheses is, border districts are having less inter-district population movements in comparison to non-border districts. The hypothesized signs and observed correlation coefficients are given in Table 6.10.

Table 6.10 shows the estimated correlation coefficients for net inter-district (male) in-migration model (NIDM; 1971, 1981). The table reveals a few of the coefficients are significantly correlated and some of them are having opposite signs to the hypothesis.

**TABLE 6.10**

**Hypothesized Signs and Observed Correlation Coefficients of Net Inter-District (Male) In-Migration Model NIDM (1971, 1981)**

| *S.No.* | *Explanatory variables* | *Hypothesized Signs* | *Estimated correlation coefficient with NIDM* | |
|---|---|---|---|---|
| | | | *1971* | *1981* |
| 1. | DP | ? | + 0.06 | - 0.23 |
| 2. | SB | - | + 0.41* | + 0.23 |

*(cont.)*

1. B.C. Mehta (1978) has attempted to calculate net migration of districts from marriage data and survival ratio. This analysis gives only an indication of economic, demographic for marriage and family in-migration but not the exact picture of in-migration.

| S.No. | Explanatory variables | Hypothesized Signs | Estimated correlation coefficient with NIDM 1971 | 1981 |
|---|---|---|---|---|
| 3. | CA | + | + 0.01 | + 0.05 |
| 4. | OU | ? | - 0.09 | - 0.15 |
| 5. | PD | + | + 0.01 | + 0.05 |
| 6. | D | - | - 0.07 | - 0.6 |
| 7. | ED | + | - 0.06 | + 0.04 |
| 8. | TP | + | + 0.08 | + 0.10 |
| 9. | ID | + | + 0.40* | + 0.44* |
| 10. | MF | + | + 0.16 | + 0.10 |
| 11. | WR | ? | - 0.02 | - 0.01 |
| 12. | MECA | + | + 0.22 | + 0.44* |
| 13. | AGO | + | + 0.48* | + 0.30 |
| 14. | BAC | + | + 0.23 | + 0.21 |
| 15. | SMR | + | + 0.47* | + 0.58* |
| 16. | AA | + | - 0.02 | + 0.02 |
| 17. | LIV | ? | - 0.27 | + 0.02 |
| 18. | AL | ? | - 0.15 | + 0.04 |
| 19. | DV | + | + 0.16 | + 0.08 |
|  | N | 26 | 26 | 26 |

Critical value (1 Tail, .05) = + or - (.33)
(2 Tail, .05) +/- (.39)
* 5% level of significance.

Corresponding results of step-wise regression estimates for the two census periods 1971 and 1981 are given in Table 6.11.

The estimated regression coefficients of the equation 6.11.1 for 1971 exhibit the hypothesized signs except the variable social backwardness (SB). Contrary to the hypotheses districts with larger proportion of backwardness (SC/ST) have attracted more net in-migrants. It may be due to the recent development of these districts. The equation explains the 92 per cent variation in the dependent variable.

**TABLE 6.11**

**Coefficients and "t" Values Obtained in Estimating Regression Equations for Net Inter-District (Male) Model, NIDM, (1971 & 1981)**

| *S.No.* | *Equation No. Variables Dep Exp* | *(6.11.1) NIDM 1971* | *(6.11.2) NIDM 1981* | *(6.11.3) NIDM (1971+1981)* |
|---|---|---|---|---|
| 1 | 2 | 3 | 4 | 5 |
| 1. | DP | — | — | — |
| 2. | SB | 0.0326** (2.12) | 0.0358*** (1.95) | 0.0391* (2.80) |
| 3. | CA | — | — | — |
| 4. | DU | — | - 0.0593** (2.68) | - 0.0506* (3.00) |
| 5. | PD | 0.0278** (2.18) | 0.0659* (3.75) | 0.0223** (2.37) |
| 6. | D | - 0.0174** (2.27) | - 0.0179*** (1.61) | — |
| 7. | ED | 2.6484* (3.80) | — | 0.7911** (1.58) |
| 8. | TP | 0.7923 (1.23) | — | — |
| 9. | ID | 0.2046*** (1.43) | 0.6217* (3.02) | 0.5853* (4.57) |
| 10. | MF | — | — | — |
| 11. | WR | - 0.1833*** (1.98) | - 0.5915 (1.58) | - 0.1412 (1.03) |
| 12. | MECA | 0.3093* (2.86) | — | — |
| 13. | AGO | 0.6765* (2.71) | — | 0.7875* (3.32) |

*(cont.)*

| 1 | 2 | 3 | 4 | 5 |
|---|---|---|---|---|
| 14. | BAC | 0.7965***<br>(1.51) | 0.5967<br>(1.13) | — |
| 15. | SMR | 5.3141*<br>(5.14) | 12.8560**<br>(2.08) | 2.2820**<br>(2.64) |
| 16. | AA | 0.2050*<br>(2.75) | — | — |
| 17. | LIV | - 0.8898**<br>(1.94) | 1.2425*<br>(2.02) | — |
| 18. | AL | - 0.3192*<br>(3.46) | — | — |
| 19. | DV | — | — | — |
| 20. | DVT | | | |
| | Constant | - 1.3305 | - 1.5521 | - 1.8489 |
| | $R^2$ | 0 .9198* | 0.7933* | 0.6493* |
| | $\overline{R}^2$ | 0.8177 | 0.6770 | 0.5840 |
| | F-value | 9.012 | 6.823 | 9.950 |
| | N | 26 | 26 | 52 |

The figures in parentheses below the regression coefficients are respective values.

Level of significance—

* 1%

** 5%

*** 10%

The equation 6.11.2 for 1981 in Table 6.11 explains 79 per cent variation in the dependent variable, NIDM. Like 1971, the signs of the estimated regression coefficients are in accordance to the expected signs except SB. The common variables in the estimation of equations for both the periods under consideration are Social Backwardness (SB), Prospective Development (PD), Distance (D), Industrial Development (ID), Water Resources (WR), Banking and Credit (BAC), Stock of Migrants (SMR) and Development of Livestock (LIV) with different level of significance. The Prospects of Development (PD), Industrial Development (ID), Banking and Credit development (BAC), Mechanization of Agriculture (MECA), prior migrants in the destination area (SMR) increase in-migration to the districts. In contrast, Water Resource (WR) availability and Degree of Urbanization (DU) reduce net in-migration to the districts. The negative sign of the variable Distance (D) shows increase in distance hampers in-migration more than out-migration in the districts of Rajasthan.

The dummy variables DV does not enter in the analysis of both the equations, which supports the null hypothesis of no difference in the pattern of net male in-migration in border and non-border districts.

In the analysis of pooled data, in the equation 6.11.3, non-entry of temporal dummy variable DVT points out no structural shift in net inter-district in-migration pattern in 1981 in comparison to base year, 1971. However, many additional variables enter in 1971 model in comparison to the 1981 model. With this, the significance of many of the explanatory variables has declined.

## 6.4 CONCLUSION

In this Chapter, linear statistical regression models are built for the male population of the 26 districts of the state. The reason for male in-migration is that it is expected to be for economic reasons whereas female migration is mostly demographic for marriage and child birth. Hypothesis are formulated on the basis of past studies and theory and they are tested by the procedure of stepwise regression analysis.

In all the four district in-migration models (DM, DME, DMRR and DMRU for male population of 26 districts of Rajasthan for 1971 and 1981. Zero-order correlation matrices for the explanatory variables in 1971 and 1981 show that the problem of multi-collinearity is not likely to arise. Stepwise regression analysis is adopted to estimate the regression coefficients, which also takes care of multi-collinearity.

In decadal in-migration of district model (DM), among SMR (the Stock Migrant Variable) is the most important variable. That is, the migrants are attracted to those destination places which are inhabited by earlier migrants from the same region of origin. Other statistically significant variables are Prospective Development of the district (PD), Industrial Development (ID), certainty of Water Resources (WR) and Degree of Urbanization (DU), which show that the prospective migrants move for the betterment of their prospects.

The explanatory power of the decadal district in-migration model is reduced when intra-district in-migration (Male), DME is excluded. It is reduced more in 1971 than in 1981 which points out short distance (intra-district) migration is in a sizeable quantity in decadal district in-migration, and dominates in each and every migration stream.

Separate models are estimated for rural-rural and rural-urban decadal in-migration. In decadal district (male) inmigration model from rural to rural areas (DMRR), the important and statistical significant variables are Prospective Development (PD), Stock of Migrants (SMR), availability of Water Resources (WR), Average Age of the population (AA), Education Development (ED). The rural to rural in-migration is related to amenities in destination place in comparison to origin place. PD i.e. the biased government expenditure in destination area increases the chances of economic betterment. SMR variable makes easier for the new migrants to adjust in the new circumstances other variables are responsible for providing better amenities and facilities. Even from the rural sector, younger and educated male population is more mobile in comparison to old people.

Decadal district rural to urban district in-migration model (DMRU) is built due to rural urban differences and this movement would prevail till these differences continue. The important variables found are Industrial Development (ID), Degree of Urbanization (DU), Banking and Credit (BAC) and Prospective

Development (PD). ID, BAC and PD increase the chances of job opportunity and DU provides the amenities of life. But the distance variable with its negative effect hampers the positive effect of these variables which points out migrants prefer to settle in the districts near their origin place. Industrial Development variable is highly significant in both the census periods 1971 and 1981, which show, districts at higher level of industrial development are the centres of attraction for the migrants.

Lastly, net inter-district migration model is built to emphasize the variables which affect in-migration and out-migration of the districts. Industrial development (ID), Education Development (ED), Mechanization of Agriculture (MECA), availability of Agricultural Output (AGO) etc. act as pull forces whereas the shortage of Water Resources (WR) and other facilities act as push forces for the migrants. The information from the friends and relatives (SMR) also contributes in the migratory movement. Distance (D) variable is significant in both the census periods 1971 and 1981, which points out to the attraction of the contiguous districts to the migrants. The dummy variable (DV) is not entered in the analysis in both the periods under consideration, which shows no regional disparity in case of net in-migration of males. The temporal dummy variable (DVT) even does not enter in the analysis, which shows no structural shift in the analysis of decadal inter-district net in-migration (males) in 1981 in comparison to 1971 census period.

In all these five district in-migration models, the temporal dummy variable (DVT) is introduced for the pooled data of 1971 and 1981 to have a glance at the structural shift in the census periods under consideration. It is significant only in case of rural to rural in-migration and rural to urban in-migration. No structural change is observed in the model of decadal district in-migration even when intra-district in-migration is excluded from it and in the net inter-district migration model.

The overall results of all the five models are satisfactory.

# 7

# *Inter-District Decadal Population (Male) Transactions Model*

The models built in Chapter-VI explain the inter-district differences in migration movements due to disparity in the explanatory variables. They do not give clear indication of the relative strength of pull and push forces in each district. This chapter is also concerned with the differences in inter-district migration movements. To analyse the relative pull and push forces, two districts (i and j) are taken at a time and the ratio of value of the each individual explanatory variable (jth/ith) is computed. The out-migration model for ith district is built which in a way is also a in-migration model of jth district. Since pull forces are decomposed into retention and attraction forces and push forces into expulsion and repulsion forces[1]. The computed ratio of each individual variable gives an indication of relative position of pull and push forces in two districts (i and j). If the value of independent variable increases, it is relative pull force which is increasing i.e. out-migration from ith district increases which in a way is the increase in in-migration of jth district and vice versa.

Like the previous chapter, this chapter again focuses on the male in-migration of the districts as the female in-migration is mainly demographic for marriage and child birth, whereas male in-migration is economic in nature.

---

1. King, J. 1978.

The chapter is organized into four sections. Section 7.1 specifies the model and defines the variables. In Section 7.2, inter-district decadal population (male) transaction model is analysed and Section 7.3 deals inter-district cluster (male) population transactions. Section 7.4 concludes the chapter.

Linear regression model is specified:

$$Mij/ni = b_1 + b_2xi_2 + b_3xi3 + ...... + b_nx_{in} + e_i$$

DPT = Mij/ni — Decadal district (male) population movement from ith to jth district i.e. male out-migration rate from ith to jth district. X's are the independent variables and $e_i$ is disturbance term with the standard assumptions of classical linear regression model.

The hypothesis regarding the relation of the explanatory variables with the dependent variables in this model are the same as those of the earlier models, the difference is only that these variables are the ratios and represent the relative pull/ push forces.

The *methodology* adopted for analysis is zero-order correlation matrix and stepwise regression analysis. Table A-7.1 (Appendix) gives the zero-order correlation matrix between the explanatory variables, it shows that no serious problem of multi-collinearity. In some cases, collinearity is relatively high, but even that is less than the overall multiple correlation coefficient. So the problem of multi-collinearity is not likely to be harmful in the present exercise[1]. Stepwise regression also takes care of the problem of multi-collinearity. This is attempted in the present exercise, the inclusion/exclusion criterion is F=1.0, only results at the last step are reported.

The variables included in the model are given in Table 7.1. Following are the ratios of the explanatory variables.

1. Klein (1969; 102).

*Dependent Variable* - Mij/ni (DPT) - the male out-migration (all types) from i to j district divided by the male population of the ith district i.e. the male out-migration rate of the ith district.

**TABLE 7.1**

**Definition of Variables used in Inter-District Migration Models**

| *S.No.* | *Explanatory variable* | *Acronym* | *Definition of variable* |
|---|---|---|---|
| 1. | DPj/DPi | (DP′) | density of population of jth district divided by the density of population of the ith district. |
| 2. | SBj/SBi | (SB′) | the ratio of the proportion of scheduled castes and tribes in total population of the jth and ith districts. |
| 3. | CAj/CAi | (CA′) | the ratio of the number of capital towns in jth and ith districts. |
| 4. | DUj/DUi | (DU′) | the ratio of the degree of urbanization of the jth and ith districts. |
| 5. | PDj/PDi | (PD′) | the ratio of the per capita plan expenditure in the jth and ith districts. |
| 6. | Dij | (D) | the distance in kilometres. The shortest road route from the jth to ith district. |
| 7. | EDj/EDi | (ED′) | the ratio of the index of educational development in the jth and ith districts. |
| 8. | IDj/IDi | (ID′) | the ratio of the index of industrial development in jth and ith districts. |
| 9. | MFj/MFi | (MF′) | the ratio of the medical facilities in the jth and ith districts. |
| 10. | TPj/TPi | (TP′) | the ratio of the transport index in the jth and ith districts. |
| 11. | WRj/WRi | (WR′) | the ratio of the water resource index of the jth and ith districts. |

*(cont.)*

| *S.No.* | *Explanatory variable* | *Acronym* | *Definition of variable* |
|---|---|---|---|
| 12. | MECAj/ MECAi | (MECA′) | the ratio of the index of mechanization in agriculture in the jth and ith districts. |
| 13. | AGOj/AGOi | (AGO′) | the ratio of the index of agricultural output in the jth and ith districts. |
| 14. | BACj/BACi | (BAC′) | the ratio of the index of banking and credit in the jth and ith districts. |
| 15. | AAj/AAi | (AA′) | the ratio of the average age in the jth and ith districts. |
| 16. | SMRj/SMRi | (SMR′) | the ratio of the stock of migrants in the jth and ith districts. |
| 17. | LIVj/LIVi | (LIV′) | the ratio of the number of livestock in the jth and ith districts. |
| 18. | ALj/ALi | (AL′) | the ratio of the per cent agricultural labour in the jth and ith districts. |
| 19. | Dummy Variable | (DV) | DV=0 for the border districts DV=1 otherwise. |
| 20. | Temporal Dummy Variable | (DVT) | DVT=0 for the Base Year and DVT=1 for 1981. |

Hypothesized signs alongwith the estimated correlation coefficients are given in Table 7.2.

Table 7.2 reveals that only some of the correlation coefficients in the inter-district population transaction model (DPT, 1971, 1981) are statistically significant and a few of them do not have sign in accordance with the formulated hypothesis. This may be due to the interaction of the explanatory variables. The real relation between dependent and independent variables can be revealed by the stepwise regression analysis. These estimated results are given in Table 7.3.

The results of log-linear specification of the model is also given in Table 7.3. For the structural change, temporal dummy variable (DVT) is included with 1971 as the Base Year (DVT=0)

**TABLE 7.2**

**Hypothesized Signs and Estimated Correlation Coefficients of Inter-District Population Transaction Model, DPT (1971, 1981)**

| *S. No.* | *Explanatory Variable* | *Hypothesized sign* | *Estimated correlation co-efficient with DPT* 1971 | 1981 |
|---|---|---|---|---|
| 1. | DP′ | ? | - 0.042 | - 0.017 |
| 2. | SB′ | - | + 0.055 | - 0.042 |
| 3. | CA′ | + | - 0.032 | + 0.104 |
| 4. | DU′ | ? | - 0.132* | + 0.010 |
| 5. | PD′ | + | + 0.037 | + 0.027 |
| 6. | D′ | - | - 0.059 | - 0.119 |
| 7. | ED′ | + | + 0.079* | + 0.038 |
| 8. | TP′ | + | + 0.063 | + 0.014 |
| 9. | ID′ | + | + 0.061 | + 0.063 |
| 10. | MF′ | + | + 0.088* | + 0.011 |
| 11. | WR′ | ? | + 0.035 | - 0.032 |
| 12. | MECA′ | + | - 0.045 | + 0.099* |
| 13. | AGO′ | + | + 0.011 | + 0.035 |
| 14. | BAC′ | + | + 0.091* | + 0.071* |
| 15. | AA′ | + | + 0.001 | + 0.050 |
| 16. | SMR′ | + | + 0.089* | + 0.024 |
| 17. | LIV′ | ? | - 0.022 | + 0.052 |
| 18. | AL′ | ? | + 0.027 | - 0.080 |
| 19. | DV | + | + 0.102* | + 0.054 |
| | n | | 650 | 650 |

Critical value (1 Tail, .05) + or - (0.063)
(2 Tail, .059 = +1 - (0.075)
* denotes 5% level of significance. Sign ? refers to open-ended hypotheses.

**TABLE 7.3**

**Co-efficient and "t" Values Obtained in Estimating Regression Equations for Decadal District Population (Male) Transaction Model, DPT (1971, 1981)**

| S.No. | Equation No. Variables | 7.3.1 | 7.3.2 | 7.3.3 | 7.3.4 | 7.3.5 | 7.3.6 |
|---|---|---|---|---|---|---|---|
| | Dep | *D P T* | | *L N D P T* | | *D P T* | *L N D P T* |
| | Exp | *1971* | *1981* | *1971* | *1981* | *(1971+1981)* | *(1971+1981)* |
| 1. | DP′ | - 0.0060* (2.690) | — | 0.2669* (2.68) | 0.1875* (2.95) | - 0.0041*** (1.89) | — |
| 2. | SB′ | — | - 0.0093 (1.23) | -3.618** (2.18) | — | - 0.0064 (1.14) | — |
| 3. | CA′ | — | — | — | — | 0.0206** (1.94) | — |
| 4. | DU′ | - 0.0232* (-2.02) | - 0.0189 (-1.39) | - 0.4366* (3.32) | 0.2351* (3.44) | 0.0157*** (1.84) | — |
| 5. | PD′ | — | — | 0.2924* (4.05) | — | — | 0.2745* (3.41) |
| 6. | ED′ | — | — | — | — | — | 0.0505 (1.21) |
| 7. | TP′ | — | — | — | — | — | 0.2050* (5.57) |

*(cont.)*

| S.No. | Equation No. Variables | 7.3.1 | 7.3.2 | 7.3.3 | 7.3.4 | 7.3.5 | 7.3.6 |
|---|---|---|---|---|---|---|---|
| | Dep | D P T | | L N D P T | | D P T | L N D P T |
| | Exp | 1971 | 1981 | 1971 | 1981 | (1971+1981) | (1971+1981) |
| 8. | ID′ | — | — | - 0.3813* (3.50) | 0.1455* (3.29) | — | 0.2010* (3.71) |
| 9. | MF′ | — | — | 0.0998 (1.05) | — | — | — |
| 10. | WR′ | — | — | 0.8262* (4.79) | - 0.2993* (2.59) | — | 0.0839 (1.20) |
| 11. | MECA′ | — | — | 0.1430 (1.85) | - 0.1785** (1.76) | — | — |
| 12. | AGO′ | 0.0091*** (1.38) | — | — | — | — | — |
| 13. | BAC′ | — | 0.0053 (1.09) | 0.5886* (4.51) | — | 0.0049 (1.34) | — |
| 14. | SMR′ | 0.0346* (4.13) | 0.1034 (3.83) | 0.1972 (1.67) | 0.6699 (4.86)* | 0.0504* (4.94) | — |
| 15. | AA′ | 0.1643** (1.91) | — — | 3.1496* (4.51) | 0.4949** (1.10) | 0.0971 (1.20) | 0.9259* (2.79) |
| 16. | LIV′ | 0.351* (3.15) | - 0.0236 (1.097) | — | — | 0.0223*** (1.86) | 0.1714* (2.89) |

*(cont.)*

| S.No. | Equation No. Variables | 7.3.1 | 7.3.2 | 7.3.3 | 7.3.4 | 7.3.5 | 7.3.6 |
|---|---|---|---|---|---|---|---|
| | Dep | D P T | | L N D P T | | D P T | L N D P T |
| | Exp | 1971 | 1981 | 1971 | 1981 | (1971+1981) | (1971+1981) |
| 17. | AL′ | — | 0.0496***<br>(1.58) | 0.2470**<br>(2.82) | 0.2490**<br>(2.03) | — | — |
| 18. | D | - 0.0053**<br>(-1.75) | - 0.0178*<br>(3.52) | - 0.3792*<br>(9.58) | - 1.4249*<br>(19.06) | - 0.112**<br>(2.41) | - 1.0201*<br>(17.79) |
| 19. | DV | 0.0658*<br>(2.99) | 0.0407<br>(1.15) | 0.5427*<br>(4.51) | 0.3475*<br>(3.08) | 0.0631*<br>(3.78) | 0.3539*<br>(4.51) |
| 20. | DVT | — | — | — | — | 0.0499*<br>(2.94) | 0.2609*<br>(3.69) |
| | Constant | - 0.0455 | 0.1090 | - 3.1850 | - 1.6263 | 0.0158 | - 2.3538 |
| | $R^2$ | 0.0768 | 0.0554* | 0.2301* | 0.4158* | 0.0571* | 0.2536* |
| | $\bar{R}^2$ | 0.0638 | 0.0436 | 0.2138* | 0.4067 | 0.0490 | 0.2478 |
| | F Ratio | 5.913 | 4.697 | 14.108 | 45.480 | 7.091 | 43.797 |
| | N | 650 | 650 | 650 | 650 | 1300 | 1300 |

"t" values are in brackets.

The equation 7.3.1 for 1971 explains only 8 per cent variation in the dependent variable. The signs of all the estimated regression coefficients are according to hypothesis formulated. The important variables in the equation are Density of Population (DP′), Degree of Urbanization (DU′), Stock of Migrants (SMR′), Development of Livestocks (LIV′) and Dummy Variable (DV).

The equation 7.3.2 for 1981 explains 5 per cent variation in the dependent variable. All the included variables exhibit the hypothesized effects. The important variables in the equation are SMR′ and D. The common significant explanatory variables in the two equations (7.3.1 and 7.3.2) are DU′, SMR′, LIV′, D and DV. The variable DV is significant at 1 per cent level of significance in 1971 and in 1981 in log-linear specification. It points to the fact that inter-district population transactions of border districts with other districts in state were small. However, with the gradual integration, difference between the pattern of border and non-border districts has diminished. The negative sign of the coefficient of Degree of Urbanization (DU′) implies, due to diseconomies of urbanization, migration decreases. Prior migrants (SMR′) act as pull force. With the development of livestock (LIV′), income of the people rises, they diversify their jobs and, therefore, the migratory movements rise. The negative sign of the distance points out that the migrants prefer the districts at short distance.

The equations 7.3.3 and 7.3.4 are present results of estimates of log-linear model in two periods under consideration. Linear and log-linear results are not directly comparable in Table 7.3. But the residual sum of squares in the two sets of equations can be compared[1]. While applying the test, it is found, the sum of squares of residuals in equations 7.3.3 and 7.3.4 are less than the equations 7.3.1 and 7.3.2 respectively. Moreover,

1. Raw & Miller, 108

in log-linear specification parameter, estimates are the elasticities and they can be compared. Hence, the log-linear function appears empirically more appropriate than the linear function for inter-district population transaction model. The fits are vastly improved, $\overline{R}^2$ jumps from 0.0638 to 0.2301 in 1971. In 1981, it is from 0.0436 to 0.4067. All $\overline{R}^2$'s are significant at 1 per cent level of significance.

In 1971 (equation 7.3.3), important variables are the Density of Population (DP′), Degree of Urbanization (DU′), Prospective Development (PD′), availability of Water Resources (WR′), Banking and Credit facilities (BAC), Average age of the population (AA′), Distance between the two districts (D) and dummy variable for border and non-border districts (DV). In equation (7.3.4), the Density of Population (DP′), Degree of Urbanization (DU′), availability of Medical Facilities (MF′), availability of Water Resources (WR′), Stock of Migrants (SMR′), the distance between the two districts (D) and the dummy variable for border and non-border districts (DV) are the significant variables. Thus DP′, DU′, ID′, WR′, MECA′, SMR′, AA′, AL′, D′ and DV′ are the common variables in the two equations. The variable DV is significant at 1 per cent level of significance in 1971 and 1981. The regression coefficient and "t" value of DV[6] in 1981 is less than 1971, which points out the increasing integration of the border districts with other districts in the state. Still border districts have smaller transactions with other districts as compared to the non-border districts.

The temporary dummy variable (DVT) in equation 7.3.5 and 7.3.6 for the pooled data in (1971+1981) in linear and log-linear specification is significant at 1 per cent level of significance. Thus there is some structural shift in migration pattern in the census year 1981 in comparison to the 1971 census year.

## 7.2 REGIONAL INTER-DISTRICT DECADAL POPULATION (MALE) TRANSACTION MODEL 1971, 1981

In order to analyse the inter-district population transactions in Chapter V, a hypothesis is formulated that inter-district migration is confined to contiguous districts. Inter-district population transaction linkage matrix (for all types of migration stream of males) is computed for 26 districts and on the basis of migration linkage co-efficients in 26 districts, five migration clusters or regions are identified.

*Region-1*: Sri Ganganagar, Bikaner, Churu, Jhunjhunu.

*Region-2*: Alwar, Bharatpur, Swai Madhopur, Jaipur, Sikar, Ajmer and Tonk.

*Region-3*: Jaisalmer, Jodhpur, Nagaur, Pali, Barmer, Jalore, Sirohi.

*Region-4*: Bhilwara, Udaipur, Chittorgarh, Dungarpur, and Banswara.

*Region-5*: Bundi, Kota and Jhalawar.

Note : Some districts can be put in more than one cluster on the basis of their linkages coefficients.

The districts forming a cluster or region are contiguous districts and support the hypothesis that inter-district migration is confined to contiguous districts.

In this Section, an attempt is made to analyse migration between districts in each region (cluster) with the application of stepwise regression analysis.

The model specification remains as in equation (A) in the previous Section (7.1) of this chapter.

The estimated correlation coefficients (1971, 1981) for all the five clusters are given in Table 7.4.

**TABLE 7.4**

**Hypothesized Signs and Estimated Correlation Coefficients for Regional Decadal Population Transaction (DPT)(1971, 1981)**

| S.No: | Variable Exp | Hypothesized sign Dep | ESTIMATED CORRELATION COEFFICIENTS Region-1 1971 | 1981 | Region-2 1971 | 1981 | Region-3 1971 | 1981 | Region-4 1971 | 1981 | Region-5 1971 | 1981 |
|---|---|---|---|---|---|---|---|---|---|---|---|---|
| 1. | DP′ | ? | 0.01 | -0.05 | 0.18 | 0.30* | -0.14 | -0.07 | 0.14 | 0.06 | -0.02 | 0.01 |
| 2. | SB′ | - | -.07 | -0.06 | 0.07 | -0.11 | -0.11 | 0.05 | 0.14 | 0.01* | 0.20* | 0.10 |
| 3. | CA′ | + | 0.05 | 0.30* | 0.20* | 0.27* | 0.04 | 0.08 | 0.19* | 0.09 | 0.02 | 0.12 |
| 4. | DU′ | ? | 0.07 | 0.06 | 0.14 | 0.10 | -0.02 | -0.02 | -0.14 | -0.07 | -0.02 | 0.10 |
| 5. | PD′ | + | 0.18* | 0.30* | 0.13* | 0.06 | 0.05 | 0.18* | 0.04 | 0.07 | 0.01 | 0.05 |
| 6. | D | - | 0.34* | -0.37* | -0.46* | -0.39* | -0.14 | -0.07 | -0.41* | -0.28* | -0.35* | -0.35* |
| 7. | ED′ | + | 0.06 | 0.16 | 0.05 | 0.41* | 0.08 | 0.18* | 0.07 | 0.09 | 0.07 | 0.21 |
| 8. | TP′ | + | 0.03 | 0.24* | 0.27* | 0.04 | 0.05 | 0.05 | 0.04 | 0.06 | 0.05 | 0.04 |
| 9. | ID′ | + | 0.03 | 0.16 | 0.37* | 0.32* | 0.01 | 0.02 | 0.03 | 0.08 | 0.18 | 0.56* |
| 10. | MF′ | + | 0.01 | 0.06 | 0.03 | 0.02 | 0.05 | 0.10 | 0.03 | 0.08 | 0.04 | 0.03 |
| 11. | WR′ | ? | -0.05 | -0.25* | 0.12 | -0.02 | -0.01 | -0.04 | -0.04 | 0.09 | 0.32* | 0.15 |

| S.No. | *Hypothesized sign Variable Exp* | *Dep* | *ESTIMATED CORRELATION COEFFICIENTS* *Region-1* | | *Region-2* | | *Region-3* | | *Region-4* | | *Region-5* | |
|---|---|---|---|---|---|---|---|---|---|---|---|---|
| | | | *1971* | *1981* | *1971* | *1981* | *1971* | *1981* | *1971* | *1981* | *1971* | *1981* |
| 12. | MECA′ | + | 0.68* | 0.68 | 0.10 | 0.18* | 0.10 | 0.07 | 0.13 | 0.09 | 0.01 | 0.01 |
| 13. | AGO′ | + | 0.10 | 0.19* | 0.08 | 0.15 | 0.10 | 0.15* | 0.20 | 0.12 | 0.15 | 0.18 |
| 14. | BAC′ | + | 0.23* | 0.35* | 0.34* | 0.15 | 0.08 | 0.15* | 0.04 | 0.07 | 0.01 | 0.10 |
| 15. | SMR′ | + | 0.28* | 0.42* | 0.16* | 0.05 | 0.10 | 0.10 | 0.05 | 0.04 | 0.14 | 0.27* |
| 16. | AA′ | + | 0.03 | 0.03 | 0.05 | 0.01 | 0.17* | 0.06 | 0.08 | 0.02 | 0.04 | 0.01 |
| 17. | LIV′ | ? | -0.26* | -0.30* | -0.17* | -0.03 | -0.04 | -0.09 | 0.45* | 0.22* | 0.04 | 0.12 |
| 18. | AL′ | ? | 0.20* | 0.18 | 0.08 | 0.11 | 0.11 | 0.05 | 0.02 | 0.13 | -0.14 | -0.02 |
| 19. | DV | + | 0.15 | 0.07 | 0.12 | 0.12 | 0.11 | 0.16* | 0.10 | 0.04 | 0.05 | 0.02 |

* Significant at 5% level.

Table 7.4 shows the estimated correlation coefficient of the dependent and the independent variables in 1971 and 1981. The coefficient of ratio of Prospective Development (PD′), Distance (D), ratio of Mechanisation in Agriculture (MECA′), ratio of Banking and Credit facilities (BAC′), the ratio of Stock of Migrants (SMR′), the ratio of Livestock development (LIV′) and ratio of Agricultural Labour (AL′) are significant at 5 per cent level of significance in 1971 for Region-1, whereas in 1981 for the same region, the coefficient of ratio of Centres of Administration (CA′), the ratio of Prospective Development (PD′), Distance between the two districts (D), the ratio of Transport Facilities (TP′), the ratio of Water Resource availability (WR′), the ratio of Mechanization in Agriculture (MECA′), the ratio of Agricultural Output (AGO′), the ratio of Banking and Credit facilities (BAC′), the ratio of Stock of Migrants (SMR′) and the ratio of Agricultural Labour (AL′) are significant at 5 per cent level of significance. For Region-2, in 1971, the coefficients of (CA′), (PD′), (D), (TP′), (ID′), (BAC′), (SMR′), (LIV′), whereas in 1981 these are (DP′), (CA′), (D), (ED′), (ID′), (MECA′), significant at 5 per cent level of significance. For Region-3, in 1971, the coefficients significant at 5 per cent level are the ratio of the Average Age of the population (AA′) whereas in these coefficients are of (PD′), (ED′), (AGO′), (BAC′) and (DV).

For Region-4, in 1971, the coefficient of the variables significant at 5 per cent are Centres of Administration (CA′), (D), (LIV′) whereas in 1981, these are (D) and (LIV′).

For Region-5, the coefficient of (SB′), (D), (WR′), in 1971, and the coefficient of (D), (ID′), (SMR′) in 1981 are significant at 5 per cent level of significance.

The sign of social backwardness (SB′) is opposite to the expected sign which may be due to the recent development of the districts. The correlation matrix (Table A-7.1) points out the non-existence of problem of multi-collinearity.

**TABLE 7.5**

**Coefficients and "t" Values Obtained in Estimating Regression Equations for Regional Decadal Population (Male) Transactions (DPT) 1971, 1981**

| S. No. | Equation Variable | 7.5.1 | 7.5.2 | 7.5.3 | 7.5.4 | 7.5.5 | 7.5.6 | 7.5.7 | 7.5.8 | 7.5.9 | |
|---|---|---|---|---|---|---|---|---|---|---|---|
| | Dep | *Region-1* | | *Region-2* | | *Region-3* | | *Region-4* | | *Region-5* | |
| | Exp | 1971 | 1981 | 1971 | 1981 | 1971 | 1981 | 1971 | 1981 | 1971 | 1981 |
| 1. | DP′ | — | -0.1946<br>(-3.46)* | -0.0740<br>(2.32)* | — | -0.0031<br>(1.01) | -0.0078**<br>(-2.06) | — | — | — | — |
| 2. | SB′ | — | 0.1135*<br>(3.06) | 0.0277***<br>(1.44) | 0.0113**<br>(1.94) | -0.0423*<br>(1.28) | — | — | -0.0596***<br>(-1.30) | — | — |
| 3. | CA′ | 0.2028*<br>(1.27) | 0.1799*<br>(5.02) | 0.0428**<br>(2.19) | — | — | — | 0.0566*<br>(2.77) | — | — | — |
| 4. | DU′ | — | 0.491<br>(1.23) | — | — | -0.0544*<br>(3.05) | — | — | — | — | — |
| 5. | PD′ | 0.0224<br>(1.56) | 0.3861*<br>(3.14) | — | — | — | — | — | — | — | — |
| 6. | ED′ | 0.0307*<br>(1.15) | 0.0079*<br>(4.34) | — | 0.2766*<br>(3.70) | 0.0216**<br>(1.97) | 0.0871***<br>(1.61) | — | — | — | — |
| 7. | TP′ | — | — | — | — | — | — | 0.0065**<br>(1.67) | 0.3885*<br>(2.53) | 0.4535*<br>(8.73) | — |

*(cont.)*

| S. No. | Equation Variable | 7.5.1 | 7.5.2 | 7.5.3 | 7.5.4 | 7.5.5 | 7.5.6 | 7.5.7 | 7.5.8 | 7.5.9 | |
|---|---|---|---|---|---|---|---|---|---|---|---|
| | Dep | *Region-1* | | *Region-2* | | *Region-3* | | *Region-4* | | *Region-5* | |
| | Exp | 1971 | 1981 | 1971 | 1981 | 1971 | 1981 | 1971 | 1981 | 1971 | 1981 |
| 8. | ID′ | 0.0538* (2.81) | — | 0.0295* (4.79) | 0.0124** (1.75) | 0.0092 (1.10) | — | 0.0094** (1.99) | 0.0241** (1.73) | 0.0547 (1.31)** | 0.0754 (1.25) |
| 9 | MF′ | 0.0660 (2.67) | — | 0.0210** (1.69) | — | 0.0197 (1.52) | — | 0.0227*** (1.61) | — | — | - |
| 10. | WR′ | — | 0.0889** (2.37) | -0.0327 (1.11) | -0.0943 (3.46) | — | — | -0.0681** (2.04) | — | 0.4477* (3.52) | — |
| 11. | MECA′ | 0.2208* (9.73) | 0.3805* (10.79) | 0.0142* (2.52) | - | 0.0214** (1.89) | — | — | — | — | — |
| 12. | AGO′ | — | — | — | - | 0.0410** (2.09) | 0.0459* (3.12) | — | 0.3507* (2.46) | — | 0.3666* (4.87) |
| 13. | BAC′ | — | 0.1341* (3.82) | — | 0.0058** (1.71) | — | — | — | — | 0.0431 (1.15) | 0.3015* (5.33) |
| 14. | SMR′ | 0.1526* (4.88) | 0.2506* (4.02) | — | -0.0999* (3.06) | — | 0.0478** (1.97) | — | — | — | 0.5159* (4.24) |
| 15. | AA′ | 0.8858* (3.08) | 0.6555* (2.97) | — | 0.4035* (2.65) | 0.3785** (2.16) | — | 0.3337** (2.11) | — | — | -1.1170* (3.31) |
| 16. | LIV′ | 0.0464** (1.66) | — | — | -0.0322 (1.76) | -0.0290 (1.28) | -0.404 (1.05) | 0.0865*** (1.33) | | | 0.1869 (1.40) |

*(cont.)*

| S. No. | Equation Variable | 7.5.1 | 7.5.2 | 7.5.3 | 7.5.4 | 7.5.5 | 7.5.6 | 7.5.7 | 7.5.8 | 7.5.9 | |
|---|---|---|---|---|---|---|---|---|---|---|---|
| | Dep | Region-1 | | Region-2 | | Region-3 | | Region-4 | | Region-5 | |
| | Exp | 1971 | 1981 | 1971 | 1981 | 1971 | 1981 | 1971 | 1981 | 1971 | 1981 |
| 17. | AL′ | — | 0.0756*** (1.29) | — | 0.1766* (2.67) | — | — | — | 0.5075* (3.08) | — | — |
| 18. | D | -0.0622* (-3.10) | -0.0521* (-3.04) | -0.0476* (-6.52) | -0.0746* (-5.76) | -0.0080* (2.78) | -0.0069** (1.68) | 0.0314* (3.34) | -0.1678 (-5.08)* | -0.0380** (1.87) | -0.1014* (4.38) |
| 19. | DV | 0.1863** (1.94) | 0.3110* (2.79) | — | — | 0.0708** (1.84) | 0.0862 (1.45) | — | — | 0.1586*** (1.46) | — |
| | Constant | 1.0386 | 0.5162 | 0.2505 | 0.4737 | -0.2139 | 0.2337 | -0.1584 | 0.979 | 0.0232 | 1.6943 |
| | $R^2$ | 0.6559* | 0.7552* | 0.3685* | 0.4053* | 0.2056* | 0.1311 | 0.3125* | 0.2248* | 0.2762* | 0.6870* |
| | $\overline{R}^2$ | 0.6128 | 0.7114 | 0.3379 | 0.3729 | 0.1414 | 0.1000 | 0.2650 | 0.1854 | 0.2123 | 0.6491 |
| | F ratio | 15.247 | 18.427 | 12.099 | 12.494 | 3.204 | 4.224 | 6.589 | 5.704 | 4.325 | 18.109 |
| | N | 100 | 100 | 175 | 175 | 175 | 175 | 125 | 125 | 75 | 75 |

Note: The figures in parentheses below the respective regression coefficients are "t" values.

* Level of significance 1%

** Level of significance 5%

*** Level of significance 10%

Table 7.5 shows the estimated regression coefficients, and "t" values for the census periods 1971 and 1981 for all the five regions/clusters.

The explanatory value of the first region equation 7.5.1, is 0.65 i.e. 65 per cent variation in the first region population transaction is explained in 1971. The ratio of important variables are Industrial Development (ID'), Medical Facilities (MF'), Mechanisation in Agriculture (MEÇA'), Stock of Migrants (SMR'), Average Age of the population (AA'), and D. The direct dummy variable DV is also significant which shows that the intra-region migration is more pronounced in the contiguous districts. District at greater distance would attract lesser migrants in a cluster. The migrants would like to move due to the facilities and amenities available in other nearby districts or due to friends and relative effect.

In equation 7.5.2 (1981) explains the 75% of the variation in the dependent variable. The ratios of important variables in the population transactions for Region-1 in 1981 are Density of Population (DP'), Social Backwardness (SB'), Centres of Administration (CA'), Educational Development (ED'), Transport Facilities (TP'), Mechanization in Agriculture (MECA'), Banking and Credit Facilities (BAC'), Stock of Migrants (SMR'), Average Age of the population (AA'), Distance (D) and Dummy Variable (DV). Most of the variables are significant at 5 per cent level of significance and the common variables with 1971 are CA', ED', MECA', SMR', AA', D and DV. The pattern of Region-1 out-migration in 1981 is same as that of 1971.

For Region-2 in 1971 and 1981, in equation 7.5.3 and 7.5.4, the common variables are SB', ED', ID', AA', LIV' and D. The sign of SB' is opposite to the hypothesized sign in 1981 which points to the recent development of the districts. DV variable does not enter in both the equations, which points out that intra-region migration is not very strong. Low $R^2$ also confirms this fact.

The equation 7.5.5 and 7.5.6 (for 1971 and 1981, Region-3) reveal that the common variables entered are ED′, LIV′, D and DV. The equation 7.5.5 explains 20 per cent variation in the dependent variable in 1971, whereas in 1981 the equation 7.5.6 explains only 13 per cent of the variation in the dependent variation. DV variable enters in both the equations though with different level of significance. It points out to the small intra-region transactions for the two census periods under consideration.

For Region-4, the equation 7.5.7 (1971) explains 31 per cent of the variation in the dependent variable (DPT), whereas equation 7.5.8 (1981) explains the variation in the dependent variable only 22 per cent. The common variable in the two equations are Industrial Development (ID′) and Distance (D). The variable DV does not enter in the analysis of both the equations which shows the intra-region population transactions is not very strong.

For Region-5, the equation 7.5.9 (1971) explains only 28 per cent variation in the dependent variable whereas the equation 7.5.10 (1981) explains 69 per cent of the variation in the dependent variable. The common variables in the two equations are ID′, BAC′ and D. The variable DV enters in 7.5.9 (1971) equation though insignificantly and does not enter in the analysis of equation 7.5.10 (1981) which points out that with the increase in integration among the districts, no difference is between the migration pattern or border and non-border districts.

The overall analysis of all the regions is satisfactory. $R^2$ for each of the five regions is significant at 1 per cent level of significance. In 1971, high value of $R^2$ is observed in only Region-1, whereas in 1981, it has also been observed in Region-5 along with the Region-1, which points out the increasing integration among the districts of the State.

## 7.4 CONCLUSION

Whereas the previous Chapter is related to district in-migration (males) models for the census periods 1971 and 1981. This Chapter focuses on inter-district migration (males) models for the same periods.

Section 1 gives clear indication of pull and push forces. The independent variables are the ratios of in/out variables and they represent the relative pull forces, whereas the dependent variable in the model is out-migration rate, from ith district to jth district. To improve the precision in the model; simple regression model is transformed into log-linear specification. The residual sum of squares reveal, the log-linear estimation results are better than linear estimation. The important variables in this model (DPT, 1971, 1981) are degree of urbanization and stock migrants. The temporal dummy variable (DVT) enters in the analysis of pooled data and points out to the structural change in the periods under consideration. The dummy variable (DV) points out to the existence of inter-district mobility in the state, though in 1981 it has declined a little.

Section 2 deals with the regression analysis of five cluster formed in Chapter V on the basis of linkages coefficients and with the hypothesis that inter-district population transactions are confined to contiguous districts. People migrate from one district to another in a cluster due to economic reasons or due to amenities and facilities available. The distance variable points out, the closer districts are centres of more attraction. The dummy variable DV points out that intra-cluster movement is strong only in case of Cluster 1 in (1971 and 1981), in Cluster 3 in (1971) and to a little extent in (1981). Cluster 5 (1971) also shows a little tendency of intra-cluster movement.

The estimated results of this chapter are satisfactory and helpful in dealing the problems of regional disparity.

# 8

# *Summary and Conclusions*

## 8.1 SUMMARY

### 8.1.1 An Overview of Migration

Migration is the major unknown components of population estimates and forecasts. Even where fertility and mortality can be projected with reasonable accuracy, estimates and forecasts for cities and regions can not be with any degree of reliability, unless the demographer is able to forecast the probable future course of internal migration. Within a nation, migration is able to offset completely or to reinforce greatly the population change resulting from the natural increase. "Migration has been variously analysed as a long term human capital investment, as a selective response of more energetic changing distribution of economic activity and as the summation of presumably asymmetric push and pull factors associated with the individual and his environment" (Todaro; 1969).

Internal migration is involved in a variety of social, economic and political problems of a nation. It is generally regarded as an economic phenomenon, although non-economic factors also have some bearing on it. It has both positive and negative effects on the economy. On the one hand, migration is considered to be an essential factor of economic development. An economy may welcome in-migrants if it has vast waste land or resources in order to enjoy economies of scale. On the other hand, widely believed notion of essentiality of in-migration for the economy is considered nothing but an "economic fallacy", therefore, there is a need to monitor such movements.

*Objective of the Study*

The focus of the present study is on the factors which influence migratory movement. But there may be reverse case i.e. migration may also affect these factors, which is not considered in the study. It is based on the secondary data.

### 8.1.2 Literature on Mobility

There is vast literature, both descriptive and analytical—econometric, available on spatial mobility or migration. The assumption that individuals make rational decision about their place of residence explicitly or implicitly underline all of the theoretical and empirical studies on migration. The econometric literature in general supports most of the conclusions of the descriptive literature with regard to the differential responses of population sub-groups to migration opportunities. The overwhelming conclusion of all migration studies, both descriptive and econometric is that people migrate primarily for economic reasons. While distance is usually a significant intervening obstacle, its negative effect can be largely offset by sizeable income differentials, especially for the more educated migrants.

In addition to primary economic motive, people migrate (a) to improve their education or skill level (b) to escape social and cultural imprisonment in homogeneous rural areas (c) to escape from rural violence and political instability and (d) to join family and friends who had previously migrated. An individual evaluates the opportunities available to him in all locations and chooses the place which maximises his satisfaction (Levy & Wadycki; 1974).

### 8.1.3 Geo-physical and Economic Features of Rajasthan

Rajasthan is a land of diversity, regional disparity prevails in all the geographic, cultural and economic characters. The state is divided into arid, semi-arid, sub-humid and humid zone according to available water resources. Most of the area of the state is desert. It consists of 60 per cent of the total area and 40 per cent of its population. The economy of the state is predominantly agrarian. There is little modern industry, but has a large variety of mineral resources which have begun to be properly mined and organised after independence. Rajasthan is still lagging behind in Indian economy in respect of the development indices of key indicators.

***Regional Disparity in Socio-Economic Indices in Rajasthan***

In the state, all the 26 districts are not on the same level of development. Some of the factors as density of population, number of capital towns, per capita, plan expenditure, degree of urbanisation, density of roads and railways, total number of registered factories and their workers, agricultural inputs and output, banking credit and facilities etc. explain the regional variations in the state. They also reflect or influence the process of migration.

### 8.1.4. Pattern of Migration in Rajasthan

The pattern of migration in Rajasthan is not simple and uni-directional, rather it is quite complex. The sex ratio of the migrants in state reveals that female in-migration is in bulk due to demographic reasons of marriage and child birth. However, male in-migration is generally economic in nature. Short distance in-migration dominates in all intra-district, inter-district as well as inter-state migration streams. Similarly, rural to rural in-migration outnumbers all other migration streams. So far as inter-state migration is concerned, the state has more in-migrants from the contiguous states like Gujarat, Haryana, MP, UP and Punjab than from the far-away states. The same pattern is revealed in out-migration from the state. Employment is the main reason for inter-state migration. Out-migration from the state is more than in-migration to the state. This shows the relative under-development of the state in comparison to the other states in the country.

Districts of the state also show regional variation in migration process, whereas some developed districts like Sri Ganganagar, Ajmer, Pali, Sirohi etc. have above average in-migrants, the less developed districts like Bikaner, Churu, Jhunjhunu etc. have below average in-migrants.

**8.1.5 Inter-District Population Transaction Movements**

Inter-district population transaction matrix has been constructed. The transaction coefficients confirm the hypothesis that migration is confined mostly to the contiguous districts. On the basis of these coefficients, five migration clusters are identified, which show in some clusters intra-cluster linkage is strong whereas in other cases it is weak. Some districts can be put in more than one clusters. In each cluster developed district(s) is surrounded by least developed districts. The pattern of migration clusters fits very well in the pattern of development clusters.

**8.1.6 District Migration Models**

Migration is influenced by a combination of geophysical, social, economic and political factors. In order to identify the different factors and to know the relative importance of factors, model building is necessary. At the district and inter-district levels several single equation models have been specified and estimated: decadal district in-migration, decadal district excluding intra-district in-migration, total rural to rural district in-migration, total net migration of districts. All models are concerned with migration of males because male migration is predominantly for economic reasons. Female migration is for demographic for marriage and child birth reasons. Migrants move due to differences in the source and destination regions with regard to the job opportunities and other amenities and facilities. The variables: Industrial Development (ID), Education Development (ED), Transport Facilities (TP), Banking and Credit Development (BAC), availability of medical facilities (MF), Prospective Development of the district (PD), Mechanisation of Agriculture (MECA) increase in-migration in a district. If the destination place is inhabited by the prior migrants from the same origin place, then the new migrants are more likely to receive information about these regions, get temporary accommodation and feel more at home in these areas. The variable, Stock of Migrants (SMR) also plays an attractive role for migrants, whereas the shortage of Water Supply (WR), Diseconomies of Urbanisation (DU), non-availability of agricultural output act as push forces for the district. Migrants move to the place where their future appears more attractive or they are able to maximise the present value of future streams of benefits minus costs. The variable, distance (D) a proxy for migration costs—psychic, pecuniary and opportunity—plays negative role for migrants, unless the difference between the level of development of the place of origin and place of destination is very large. Migration is regarded as a long term human investment, so the young people are more likely to migrate to improve their skill or education.

### 8.1.7 Inter-District Population Movement

Inter-district population transaction model points out that most of the districts are border districts, so there is difference in the pattern of border and non-border districts. Inter-district migration is more in case of non-border districts. This difference is declining with the passage of time and integration is also increasing in the state. The transport facilities, medical facilities, banking and credit development, education development, mechanisation in agriculture, industrial developopment, availability of surplus agricultural output and the availability of water supply in the destination regions are the pull factors for migration. The distance between the districts is very important, contiguous districts attract more migrants.

The migratory behaviour within region (migration clusters) also point out that the process of movement of human population is an aspect of regional organisation.

## 8.2 CONCLUSIONS AND POLICY IMPLICATIONS

The basic premise of an economic analysis is that a rational human remains always busy to maximise his utility/minimise his disutility by allocating his constrained resources. On this line of thinking, one may observe this thesis.

Spatial mobility/migration of the people is in pursuit of the fulfilment of certain specified goals for certain period of time or on permanent basis. These specified goals may be related with push factors at the original place of residence or to pull factors operation at the intended place of residence. Migration is thus a response of human organism to economic, social and demographic forces in the economy.

In this thesis, an attempt has been made to analyse individual as well as aggregate human behaviour with the aid of economic theories and econometric instrument. The major findings of the research are as follows:

**8.2.1 Overall mobility in Rajasthan is low** in comparison with other states of India. In 1971 census, it was only 29.76 per cent of the total population while in 1981 census the figure is only 29.80 per cent. The decadal increase in mobility is very negligible. It points out the relative low development of the state.

**8.2.2 The basic pattern of inter-regional population flow is not simple and unidirectional.** Four migration streams, rural to rural, rural to urban, urban to urban and urban to rural are prevailing in the state. Rural to rural and rural to urban areas are the two important migration streams. Rural to rural migration stream has declined over time due to initial process of balanced development but is still a dominant stream. Rural to urban migration has rising trend. Even urban to urban and urban to rural movements are rising in 1981 census in comparison with 1971 census. The inter-regional longer-distance flows tend to be dominated by men, whereas the shorter-distance flows are female dominated. Male migration is for economic reasons and female migration is demographic for marriage and child birth, indicated by the relatively high sex ratio (females per 1000 males).

**8.2.3 Net out-migration from the state is more than net in-migration in the state.** The people generally move to contiguous states like UP, MP and Gujarat for economic reasons. This also points out the relative low development of the state.

**8.2.4 There is large regional variation in migration pattern of the state.** Developed districts like Ganganagar, Bikaner, Jaipur and Ajmer are more attractions for migrants than the less developed districts like Jaisalmer, Barmer and Jalore. Inter-regional population transaction matrix reveals, migration is confined to contiguous districts which are culturally homogeneous. Distance is main impediment for movement.

**8.2.5 The pattern of migration** in the state in the two census periods 1971 and 1981 is same. No structural change has occurred in the state. The coefficient of correlation between the two is (.82). The pace of change is very low in the state.

**8.2.6 The regional disparity prevails** in all the key indicators of development, such as in the level of education (27.32, 93.00)*, industrial development (93.00, 99.82), transport and infrastructural facilities (38.00, 56.48), medical facilities (44.99, 69.86), availability of water resources (110.00, 41.92), mechanisation in agriculture (145.00, 83.18), availability of agricultural output (50.00, 46.40), even the government expenditure in the development of the districts is lopsided (104.00, 87.05). The indicators government expenditure, mechanisation in agriculture and availability of water resources indicate high variation in 1971 while in 1981 they have shown a declining trend, which show that with the efforts of the

---

*C.V. (%) in 1971 and 1981 respectively.

government, regional imbalances have started to decline, whereas indicators such as education development, infrastructural development, medical facilities have shown large inter-regional variation even in 1981.

There was a decrease in inequalities in the past, but a change may also be expected in the near future.

**8.2.7 Rajasthan is a backward state** in comparison with other states. It is having low rank in the economic indices among the states covered e.g. in per capita income (18th) among the 24 states, in literacy rate (22nd) among the 22 states in infrastructural development (17th) among the 24 states, in per capita expenditure on education (21st) among 25 states.[1]

**8.2.8** Since migratory movement is influenced by a combination of geophysical and socio-economic differences in the districts, on the basis of past theories and generalisations different district and inter-district migration models have been built. They confirm the validity of size-distance theories (gravity models), push-pull theories (regression models) and probabilistic theories (probit models). The results indicate that there are some conditions like lack of infrastructural facilities or lack of development of education and medical facilities that exert pressure on people to move out. The results of rural to urban migration fully confirm the Todaro model that rural to urban in-migration is due to rural-urban differences in economic opportunities.

These conclusions of this thesis provide useful insight, for development policy to the policy-makers.

## POLICY IMPLICATIONS

Public policy is a mechanism for realising social goals. The crux of the process is that it provides a valid reflection of

---

1. CMIE (1989) *Basic Statistics Relating to Indian Economy.*

the goals and priorities of citizens. Public policy development in the end involves three operational activities—goal settlement, resource allocation and evaluation of effectiveness.

The results of this research point out that overall mobility in the state is low. In fact, the inter-relationships between development and migration are complex and complicated. For the development of the state, people should be more mobile. Migrants are dynamic, risk bearing persons and detach themselves from the traditional surroundings.[1] They are productive from the point of view of economic growth. So the mobility of the people should increase. But this is not a spontaneous process. Efforts from the government are needed to spread information concerning opportunities in other areas. As distance is main impediment in migration, there should be well developed network of roads and railways combined with subsidised transport. This would increase the mobility of the people.

The results indicate in the four migration streams, rural to rural stream is a dominant stream. This migration is due to the natural increase of population of rural areas, that has led to out-migration from rural areas as it has led much pressure on the resources of agricultural land. This migration is also governed by different level of agricultural wages. All these factors should be quantified and analysed in order to understand the pattern of rural to rural migration in the state.

Rural to urban migration is only next to rural to rural. It is inevitable rather concomitant in the process of development. This migration stream is likely to increase the different socio-economic problems of urban areas particularly of public utilities like housing, water facilities, medical facilities etc. So there should be master plan for the major cities and their surroundings. Steps should also be taken for the framing of policies on such issues as amount of resources to be allocated

1. Kuznets (1966).

to the development of existing towns and new urban places, the development of economic base of these towns and the way in which they are to be integrated with one another and with their surrounding areas. Failure to evolve such guidelines in the near future could lead to irreversible structural changes which will be detrimental to development as a whole.

To monitor rural to urban movements, manufacturing industries should be based on agricultural produce. Emphasis should be given for setting up new industries and other commercial and professional establishments in rural places taking advantage of the particular special conditions available. It is observed from the scheme of urban development that very little attention has been paid to the issues relating to rural-urban migration beyond the question of relieving population pressure of the metropolises, although it is recognised that urban development should be seen as complementary to rural development and policies governing the process of urbanisation should be such as to strengthen the links between town and cities and their surroundings so that the former serve the rural areas more efficiently.

The results point out that urban to urban and urban to rural migration is also increasing. From the mobility point of view and consideration of economic development, this may prove to be a healthy trend, but there is a need to understand the pattern of this migration more clearly.

With the increase in mobility, floating population is likely to increase. So there is a need to shift migrants from the overcrowded areas to sparsely populated areas. This transference of population depends on certain preconditions such as governmental investment in the establishment of basic infrastructural such as housing, roads, education and health facilities, proper administration etc. The emphasis should be on the need to prevent the unrestricted growth of metropolitan cities and there should be a regional approach to solve the problem of urbanisation and human settlement.

In the state, regional disparity prevails in socio-economic indices and in the inter-regional migration pattern. It is necessary that hitherto less developed districts should be given more attention. Arid and semi-arid regions should be given priority in the development plans of the state.

With all these efforts from the state government, there may be balanced development of the state and which may weaken the prevailing push forces. To implement these suggestions, a long-term planning is needed at the state level. There should be active migration policy. It should not be formulated in isolation but should be integrated with the policy of economic development of the state.

## 8.3 LIMITATIONS

Following are some of the limitations of the study.

### 8.3.1. Based on Census Data

This is a census based study, the degree of accuracy and coverage of census data may vary greatly from one census to the next. Moreover, census data quickly become outdated with socio-economic conditions. But field survey studies also have a number of inherent weaknesses.

### 8.3.2 Single Equation Models are Developed

Migration is influenced by multiplicity of causes, which may themselves be dependent on migrations. This necessitates the building of simultaneous equation model.Ideally the process of migration should be examined in the context of a general equilibrium system and not just a partial framework implied in a single equation model. Such an attempt has not been made in the study. So the OLS estimates based on the single equation will create the problem of simultaneity bias. However, development of a simultaneous equation model would have required development of a full demographic-economic interaction model of the state. This exercise has been left for future research.

**8.3.3 The Data Used**

The data used are *highly aggregated* and the model cannot be used to describe individual person's behaviour. Error may arise due to this aggregation. In the study, individual migration behaviour has been analysed on the basis of cross-district differences in geo-physical and socio-economic differences.

**8.3.4 Weak Data Base**

Any comprehensive and intellectual approach to the study of underlying causes of inter-regional population movements must inevitably recognise and deal with numerous little understood relationships among economic, sociological, demographic and political variables. But this task is hampered by a severe shortage of accurate data required for the useful work on the problem. This problem is common to LDC's (Mitra). Attempt has been made to minimise errors in the study while choosing proxies for variables included in the model.

**8.3.5** The study attempts to explain the factors causing migration, the *effects of migration and the consequences of differential and return migration are* not examined in the study.

Despite its many shortcomings, the approach to migration determinants employed in this study broadly corroborates the view of migration as a rational economic phenomenon. A framework such as the one developed here can be a valuable tool in providing policy-makers with some insight into the nature, scope and elements of an economically rational migration policy. With population movements performing an important function in facilitating structural changes associated with the development process, policies could be framed to increase the flow of information about existing economic opportunities in different geographical regions and reduce uncertainties associated with the exploitation of these opportunities.

"Searching and learning process go hand in hand and the learning process is often reinforced by new information and experience gained from the past behaviour", (Abler, 1971). Thus, any result at this time should be regarded as necessarily preliminary. There is a field for future reseach in this direction.

# 9

# *Post-Script*

## MIGRATION IN RAJASTHAN (1991)

Migration is an important aspect in the field of population study. A community or a country can gain population by births or by in-migration and it can loose population by death among its residents or by out-migration. In other words, migration is a major factor in changing the size and structure of the population.

In every census, the scope of enquiry on migration is widened. In 1991 census, reasons of migration are widened and classification of migrants has also been done on various basis, to study the behaviour of migrants in depth. With this approach the analysis of migratory behaviour of the migrants (1991) can be done in depth but it makes the comparison with data of earlier census difficult.

Table 9.1 shows the percentage distribution of in-migrants in Rajasthan by Place of Birth.

The table 9.1 shows migrant population in the state is only 28.53 per cent. A marginal decline in the in-migrant population is observed in the 1991 migration data as compared to early census. It may be due to the more development of the neighbouring states. Male in-migration in the state is only 20.28 per cent and female in-migration due to demographic reasons is 79.72 per cent. Rural in-migration is observed 75.89 per cent and urban in-migration 24.10 per cent.

**TABLE 9.1**

**Percentage Distribution of In-Migrants in Rajasthan**
(By place of birth)

| *S. No.* | *Place of Birth* | *Persons* | *% of population* |
|---|---|---|---|
| (a) | Born in the place of enumeration | 3,16,23,322 | 71.47 |
| (b) | Born elsewhere in the district of enumeration (short distance migration) | 78,10,485 | 17.75 |
| (c) | Born in other districts of the state (medium distance migration) | 29,29,056 | 6.91 |
| (d) | Born in other states of India (long distance migration) | 14,66,134 | 3.46 |
| (e) | Born in other countries plus unclassified (international migration) | 1,76,993 | 0.41 |
| | Total Population of Rajasthan | 44,005,990 | 100.00 |

Source: Census of India, 1991, Migration Tables of Rajasthan, 1991.

Following table 9.2 shows the in-migration pattern in Rajasthan on the basis of last residence, if it is some where else than the place of enumeration.

**TABLE 9.2**

**In-migration Pattern in Rajasthan (%)**
(Based on last residence) (1991)

| | |
|---|---|
| Total migration | 28.78 |
| Total rural migration | 76 |
| Total urban migration | 24 |
| Male migration | 20.50 |
| Female migration | 79.50 |
| Intra-national migration | 99.00 |
| International migration | 1.00 |

Source: Census of India, 1991, Migration Tables of Rajasthan, 1991.

The table 9.2 shows 28.78 per cent of the total population in the state is in-migrants. In this percentage, 99 per cent is intra-national and 1 per cent international. The state, though, is less developed but still it has inmigrants from other countries. This shows future prospects of development of the state. Mostly migrants (76%) are from the rural due to less development of the rural areas and rural to rural migration may be due to disparity in the development of rural sector. Urban migration is only 24 per cent it may be due to the education, employment and business reasons. The percentage of male migration is only 20.50 because it is a economic migration, while the percentage of female migration is 79.50. The female migration is always higher than male migration because females mostly migrate due to marriage. Thus it can be concluded from table 9.1 that migration in the state may be horizontal or vertical but not much change has been observed in the total migration over the years.

**TABLE 9.3**

**Four Streams of Migration (Distance wise)**

**(A) Intra - District Migration (%)**

(Short Distance)

Total intra-district migration = 63.63 %

| | *Male* | *Female* |
|---|---|---|
| Total | 17.13 | 82.87 |
| Rural | 13.46 | 86.54 |
| Urban | 37.57 | 62.43 |
| Rural to rural | 13.04 | 86.96 |
| Rural to urban | 39.23 | 60.77 |
| Urban to rural | 19.28 | 80.72 |
| Urban to urban | 32.59 | 67.51 |

Source: Census of India, 1991, Migration Tables of Rajasthan, 1991.

**(B) Inter-district Migration (%)**
(Medium Distance)

Total inter-district migration = 23.86 %

| | *Male* | *Female* |
|---|---|---|
| Total | 23.33 | 76.67 |
| Rural | 74.45 | 85.55 |
| Urban | 38.92 | 61.08 |
| Rural to rural | 13.23 | 86.77 |
| Rural to urban | 41.13 | 58.87 |
| Urban to rural | 23.68 | 76.32 |
| Urban to urban | 36.65 | 63.35 |

Source: Census of India, 1991, Migration Tables of Rajasthan, 1991.

**(C) Inter-state Migration (%)**
(Long Distance)

Total inter-state migration = 11.60 %

| | *Male* | *Female* |
|---|---|---|
| Total | 30.11 | 69.89 |
| Rural | 20.79 | 79.21 |
| Urban | 42.31 | 57.69 |
| Rural to rural | 17.86 | 82.14 |
| Rural to urban | 45.49 | 54.51 |
| Urban to rural | 35.84 | 64.16 |
| Urban to urban | 40.15 | 59.85 |

Source: Census of India, 1991, Migration Tables of Rajasthan, 1991.

As there are four streams of migration and it may be distance wise, short, medium and long distance. Distance travelled is always obstacle to the migrants. Generally short-distance migration is more than the long distance. The table 9.3 shows four streams of migration distance wise. Short distance (intra-district) migration is 63.63 per cent of the total migration. Medium distance (inter-district) is 23.68 per cent and long distance (inter-state)is only 11.60 per cent. It is observed in the tables male migration which is mainly due to economic reasons increases with the distance, while female migration decreases. Intra-district male migration is 17.13 per cent while inter-state male migration is 30.11 per cent whereas the percentage of female migration is 82.87 and 69.89 respectively for the short and long distance. This shows females always prefer short distance migration in comparison to long distance. Rural male migration is less than urban male migration in all the distances because of the more dynamism and education in urban males whereas the percentage of rural females is more than urban females in short, medium and long distance due to marriage purpose. In the four streams of migration, rural to urban migration is higher for males and for females rural to rural migration is higher. Because male migration is economic, as more education, job and business opportunities are available in urban centres. So the rural males migrate to urban centres whereas female migration is non-economic. After rural to urban migration is urban to urban migration. This is also due to the disparity in the level of urban centres. To control this flow it is necessary policy should be formulated and implemented for the balanced development of rural and urban sectors.

Following table 9.4 shows in addition to the 1981 migration data the classification of in-migrants in the state in to main, marginal and non-workers. This shows all the in-migrants are not able to get the work.

In addition to the 1981 migration tables, in the migration data (1991), additional information is obtained in table 9.4. The table shows 52.97 per cent of the in-migrants are non-workers, i.e., they are not able to get the work anywhere, whereas 28.10 per cent are working as main workers and 18.93 per cent as marginal workers. As the percentage of female in-migrants is higher than male in-migrants. The percentage of female workers in all the three categories is

**TABLE 9.4**

**Classification of In-Migrants in to Main, Marginal and Non-Workers**

| | *Total* | *Total male* | *Total female* | *Total* | *Rural male* | *Urban female* | *Total* | *Rural male* | *Urban female* | *Total* |
|---|---|---|---|---|---|---|---|---|---|---|
| Main workers | 28.10 | 44.40 | 55.60 | 100.00 | 72.43 | 27.57 | 100.00 | 91.92 | 8.08 | 100.00 |
| Marginal workers | 18.93 | 0.92 | 99.08 | 100.00 | 83.00 | 17.00 | 100.00 | 93.88 | 6.12 | 100.00 |
| Non-workers | 52.97 | 14.82 | 85.18 | 100.00 | 71.94 | 28.06 | 100.00 | 80.17 | 19.83 | 100.00 |

Source: Census of India, 1991, Migration Tables of Rajasthan, 1991.

higher than males but the percentage of female marginal workers is higher than female main workers and non-workers. While comparing the rural and urban male in-migrant workers it is found the percentage of rural males is higher than urban males in all the three categories as the rural migration is higher than urban migration. The percentage of rural male workers is higher as marginal workers whereas the percentage of urban male workers is higher as non-workers and main workers. With regard to rural female in-migrants like rural male in-migrants the percentage is higher in all the three categories than the urban female in-migrants. The percentage of female in-migrants is higher as marginal workers. This shows in comparison to male, females are mostly employed as marginal workers and rural in-migrants in comparison to urban in-migrants mostly work as marignal workers.

In-migrants are not only literates but also illiterates. Following table 9.5 shows the classification of migrants according to literacy level. Total literate migrants are 22.86 per cent whereas the remaining percentage 77.14 is of illiterate migrants.

The percentage of literate male migrants is higher than illiterate migrants whereas the percentage of female illiterate migrants is higher than literate migrants. While comparing the rural and urban sectors. The percentage of literate and illiterate rural males is higher than urban males. Likewise the percentaage of rural literate and illiterate females is higher than urban literate and illiterate females. This is because in all the four streams of migration rural to urban migration is higher than other streams.

**TABLE 9.5**

**Classification of Migrants According to Literacy Level (%)**

| *Migrants* | *Total* | | | *Male* | | | *Female* | | |
|---|---|---|---|---|---|---|---|---|---|
| *Category* | *Male* | *Female* | *Total* | *Rural* | *Urban* | *Total* | *Rural* | *Urban* | *Total* |
| Literates | 52.96 | 47.04 | 100 | 65.74 | 34.26 | 100 | 57.51 | 42.49 | 100 |
| Illiterates | 10.87 | 89.13 | 100 | 81.84 | 18.16 | 100 | 90.13 | 9.87 | 100 |

Source: Census of India, 1991, Migration Tables of Rajasthan, 1991.

In 1991, data reasons of migration are diversified than 1981 migration data. Following table 9.6 shows the reasons of gender maigraion.

The Table 9.6 shows migrants are moving for both economic and non-economic reasons. Male migration in comparison to females is mainly due to economic reasons like employment (30.08%), business (8.04%) the education attainment is also important purpose of migration in this case for male the percentage (5.26%) is higher than females (0.42%). Female migration (84.54%) is mainly due to marriage purpose. Male migration due to marriage is very low (3.39%). To accompany with the family also shows the higher percentage (26.70%) than females (7.39%). Movement due to natural calamities also exist in the state, though it is less than 1 per cent. Even in this case male percentage (0.57) is higher than females (0.09). The percentage of male migrants (25.96) for other unspecified reasons is higher than female migrants (6.07). In the total migration highest percentage (67.90) is observed due to marriage purpose because of high female migration. To accompany with the earning member of the

**TABLE 9.6**

**Reasons of Migration (Genderwise) (1991)**

| *S.No.* | *Reasons* | *Male* | *Female* | *Total* |
|---|---|---|---|---|
| 1. | Employment | 7,81,115 (30.08 %) | 1,18,125 (1.17%) | 8,99,240 (7.09%) |
| 2. | Business | 2,08,905 (8.04%) | 39,840 (0.39%) | 2,48,745 (1.96%) |
| 3. | Education | 1,36,800 (5.26%) | 42,660 (0.42%) | 1,79,460 (1.43%) |
| 4. | Family moved | 6,93,470 (26.70%) | 7,37,809 (7.32%) | 14,31,279 (11.29%) |
| 5. | Marriage | 87,948 (3.39%) | 85,13,224 (84.54%) | 86,01,172 (67.90%) |
| 6. | Natural calamities like drought, floods etc. | 14,869 (0.57%) | 9120 (0.09%) | 23,989 (0.21%) |
| 7. | Others | 6,73,588 (25.96%) | 6,08,908 (6.09%) | 12,82,497 (10.12%) |

Source: Census of India, 1991, Migration Tables of Rajasthan, 1991.

family is also high (11.29%). Least percentage (0.21) is observed due to the natural calamities. All these reasons of migration emphasise the need of formulation of development policies accordingly so that the flow of migrants from the less developed to more developed areas could be controlled.

Following table 9.7 shows the regional distribution of migrants at district level on the basis of all duration migration.

The districts having above average in-migrants are Alwar, Bhilwara, Bikaner, Bundi, Chittorgarh, Dungarpur, Ganganagar, Jaisalmer, Jhunjhunun, Kota, Pali, Sirohi. All these districts are either industrialized or newly developed regions which are the source of attraction for new in-migrants.

**TABLE 9.7**

**Regional Distribution of Migrants**

% of total population (1991)

| S.No. | Districts | % of migrants |
|---|---|---|
| 1. | Ajmer | 27.81 |
| 2. | Alwar | 29.55 |
| 3. | Banswara | 25.40 |
| 4. | Barmer | 24.41 |
| 5. | Bharatpur | 25.76 |
| 6. | Bhilwara | 30.46 |
| 7. | Bikaner | 28.83 |
| 8. | Bundi | 30.18 |
| 9. | Chittorgarh | 35.46 |
| 10. | Churu | 27.13 |
| 11. | Dholpur | 24.99 |
| 12. | Dungarpur | 30.50 |
| 13. | Ganganagar | 39.24 |
| 14. | Jaipur | 27.92 |
| 15. | Jaisalmer | 28.12 |
| 16. | Jalore | 26.47 |
| 17. | Jhalawar | 27.58 |
| 18. | Jhunjhunun | 28.34 |
| 19. | Jodhpur | 21.33 |
| 20. | Kota | 35.16 |
| 21. | Nagaur | 26.89 |
| 22. | Pali | 28.73 |
| 23. | Sawai Madhopur | 25.70 |
| 24. | Sikar | 27.16 |
| 25. | Sirohi | 30.68 |
| 26. | Tonk | 27.09 |
| 27. | Udaipur | 26.07 |
| | Mean | 28.41 |
| | Coefficient of variation (%) | 12.67 |

Source: Census of India, 1991, Migration Tables of Rajasthan, 1991.

**Table 9.8**

**Rajasthan in Indian Economy**

| *S.No.* | *Year* | *Item* | *Unit* | *Rajasthan* | *All India* | *India Max.* | *India Min.* | *Rajasthan Rank* |
|---|---|---|---|---|---|---|---|---|
| 1. | 2 | 3 | 4 | 5 | 6 | 7 | 8 | 9 |
| **DEMOGRAPHY** | | | | | | | | |
| 1. | 1991 | Population in ('000) | Number | 44006 | 846,302 | 1391 (U.P.) | 164 (Haryana) | 9th |
| 2. | 1981 | Annual rate of growth | Percent | 2.5 | 2.1 | 2.5 (Raj., Haryana) | 1.3 (Kerala) | 2nd |
| 3. | 1991 | Density of population | Persons per sq. km. | 129 | 257 | 749 (Kerala) | 129 (Raj.) | 15th |
| 4. | 1991 | Urbanisation | Percent | 22.9 | 25.7 | 38.7 (Maharashtra) | 11.1 (Assam) | 10th |
| 5. | 1991 | Sex ratio | Female per thousand males | 910 | 929 | 1040 (Kerala) | 882 (UP) | 12th |
| 6. | 1991 | Birth rate<br>Death rate | Per thousand | 33.9<br>10.0 | 29.9<br>10.1 | 36.1 (MP)<br>13.1 (MP) | 19.1 (UP)<br>6.0 (Kerala) | 3rd<br>6th |
| **AGRICULTURE** | | | | | | | | |
| 7. | 1990-91 | NIA ('000 hec.) | Hectare | 3904 | 47434 | 10542 (UP) | 333 (Kerala) | 5th |

*cont...*

| 1 | 2 | 3 | 4 | 5 | 6 | 7 | 8 | 9 |
|---|---|---|---|---|---|---|---|---|
| 8. | 1988-89 | Share of Agriculture to NSDP | Rs. | 3604 | NA | 9172 (UP) | 1431 (Assam) | 6th |
| **INDUSTRY** | | | | | | | | |
| 9. | 1989-90 | Per capita value added by manufacturer factory sector | Rs. | 266 | 514 | 1266 (Maharashtra) | 266 (Rajasthan) | 15th |
| 10. | 1989-90 | No. of registered factories | Number | 3089 | 107,992 | 16007 (AP) | 1405 (Orissa) | 7th |
| 11. | 1988-89 | Share of Mtg. Sector to NSDP | Rs. (in Cr.) | 1269 | NA | 7842 (Maharashtra) | 824 (Assam) | 8th |
| **EDUCATION** | | | | | | | | |
| 12. | 1991 | Literacy rate | T (%)<br>M (%)<br>F (%) | 38.55<br>54.99<br>20.44 | 52.1<br>64.1<br>39.3 | 89.8 (Kerala) | 38.55 (Rajasthan) | 15th |
| **HEALTH SERVICES** | | | | | | | | |
| 13. | 1988 | Hospital and dispensary. | Number | 21788 | 609735 | 95004 (Maharashtra) | 7688 (Haryana) | 12th |
| | | Beds per lakh of population | | 64 | 89 | 292 (Kerala) | 41 (Bihar) | 10th |

*cont...*

| 1 | 2 | 3 | 4 | 5 | 6 | 7 | 8 | 9 |
|---|---|---|---|---|---|---|---|---|
| | | Hospitals and Dispensaries | Number | 1454 | 37326 | 1013 (Maharashtra) | 214 (Haryana) | 7th |
| | | per '000 sq. km. | | 4.3 | 11.4 | 106.4 (Maharashtra) | 106.4 (Orissa) | 14th |
| **TRANSPORT** | | | | | | | | |
| 14. | 1987-88 | Road length per '000 sq. km. | Km | 194 | 544 | 3173 (Kerala) | 194 (Raj.) | 15th |
| | 1992-93 | Registered motor vehicles | Number | 1,009,240 | 23,271,120 | 2,889,040 (Maharashtra) | 2,99,390 (Assam) | 11th |
| | 1992-93 | Total route | Km. | 5740 | 62486 | 8901 (UP) | 1028 (Kerala) | 3rd |
| | | length per '000 sq.km. | | 16.77 | 18.01 | 43.10 (W.B.) | 12.86 (Orissa) | |
| **POWER & ELECTRIFICATION** | | | | | | | | |
| 17. | 1989-90 | Power consumption | TKwh | 4.33 | 100.00 | 16.54 (Maharashtra) | 78 (Assam) | 11th |
| | | | D | 16.3 | 22.3 | | | |
| | | | A | 27.7 | 25.1 | | | |
| | | | 1 | 46.3 | 46.0 | | | |
| 18. | 1992-93 | Per capita consumption of electricity | Kwh | 320.0 | 330.6 | 863.1 (Punjab) | 60.7 (Bihar) | 7th |

Source: *Statistical Abstract of Rajasthan*, 1991.

Due to different level of development and density of population in the districts, the variation of in-migrants in the region is 12.67 per cent.

Migration is closely linked with the development of the region. Table 9.8 shows the position of Rajasthan in Indian Economy in 1991 in comparison to 1981.

In this table 9.8 Rajasthan is compared with 15 states of India. The rank of Rajasthan in annual population growth is 2nd equivalent to Haryana, whjich is a developed state. Lowest density of population, 15th rank is observed in the state, while in the size of population its rank is 9th which shows most of the population out migrate to the neighbouring states due to less develoment of the state. Urbanization in the state is on 10th place, basically due to rural to urban migration. Sex ratio, which shows the status of females in the state is on 12th place. The rank in the birth rate is 3rd which is linked with the high population growth rate, death rate is on 6th place. Due to development of medical and health facilities (7th rank) the state's position is healthy in comparison to neighbouring state Madhya Pradesh, which is having the highest death rate. Share of agriculture in the net state domestic product is on 6th place and of manufacturing sector 8th place. This shows agricultural sectors provides the major share of the state's domestic product. Literacy rate in the state is very low. The state is having lowest rank in 15 selected states. Road transport is not fully developed in the state, in this regard the state is having 15th rank. The 7th rank is observed in per capita consumption of electricity. All these indicators show the state is progressing as compared to other less developed states like U.P., Bihar and M.P.

On the basis of agricultural, industrial, educational and infrastructural composite index of development, an overall development index is computed in 1991. Following table 9.9 shows the classification of districts on the basis of overall development index. The ranks are given in ascending order.

**TABLE 9.9**

**Classification of Districts on the Basis of Overall Development Index (1991)**

| *S. No.* | *Range* | *Development Category* | *Districts* | *% of Districts* |
|---|---|---|---|---|
| 1. | < 7.83 | Very High | Alwar (1) | 3.86 |
| 2. | 7.83 to 10.36 | High | Jaipur, Kota, Ajmer, Udaipur (4) | 15.39 |
| 3. | 10.36 to 12.89 | Average | Pali, Sirohi, Jodhpur, Jhunjhunun, Bharatpur, Sikar, Bhilwara (7) | 26.92 |
| 4. | 12.89 to 15.42 | Low | Ganganagar, Bikaner, Chittorgarh, Nagaur, Jhalawar, Dungarpur, Bundi (7) | 26.92 |
| 5. | 15.25 < | Very Low | Banswara, Churu, Jaisalmer, Barmer, Tonk, Sawai Madhopur, Jalore (7) | 26.92 |

Source: Computed.

The table 9.9 shows 14 districts (53-84%) are on below average development. 7 districts (26.92%) on average development and only 5 districts (3.86%) are on above average development. Due to this regional difference in the level of development intra-state migration takes place. This variation is to be minimised.

## APPENDIX - 1

**District-wise Geo-physical and Socio-economic Indices, 1981**

| | DP | SB | CA | DU | PD | D | ED | TP | ID | MF | WR | MECA | AGO | BAC | SMR | AA | LIV | AL |
|---|---|---|---|---|---|---|---|---|---|---|---|---|---|---|---|---|---|---|
| 1. | 98.000 | 29.300 | 5.000 | 20.610 | 60.120 | 200.000 | 1.897 | 1.040 | 2.647 | 23.520 | 1.006 | 7.430 | 3.419 | 1.850 | 0.365 | 23.430 | 38.120 | 9.000 |
| 2. | 81.000 | 18.530 | 4.000 | 39.480 | 94.160 | 137.00 | 1.367 | 69.000 | 1.781 | 157.580 | 1.116 | 1.350 | 0721 | 2.150 | 0.160 | 22.810 | 56.170 | 3.000 |
| 3. | 70.000 | 20.030 | 1.000 | 29.220 | 7.160 | 60.000 | 1.289 | 0.710 | 0.492 | 33.780 | 1.662 | 0.910 | 1.061 | 0.650 | 0.056 | 21.960 | 34.240 | 6.000 |
| 4. | 204.000 | 16.810 | 1.000 | 20.740 | 15.610 | 52.000 | 1.984 | 1.020 | 0.442 | 28.080 | 2.195 | 1.200 | 1.561 | 0.620 | 0.051 | 24.900 | 70.320 | 6.500 |
| 5. | 211.000 | 8.760 | 3.000 | 42.600 | 10.630 | 100.000 | 2.327 | 1.320 | 0.754 | 46.300 | 2.414 | 1.930 | 3.407 | 0.079 | 0.109 | 23.490 | 70.200 | 7.000 |
| 6. | 233.000 | 3.310 | 4.000 | 17.070 | 19.210 | 126.000 | 2.711 | 1.020 | 2.489 | 33.590 | 2.156 | 2.320 | 2.968 | 0.420 | 0.091 | 23.429 | 42.240 | 7.200 |
| 7. | 146.000 | 23.040 | 2.000 | 13.420 | 15.210 | 78.000 | 1.775 | 0.990 | 2.542 | 12.560 | 2.191 | 0.950 | 3.155 | 0.520 | 0.090 | 23.740 | 50.240 | 7.000 |
| 8. | 243.000 | 11.120 | 4.000 | 36.560 | 33.160 | 88.000 | 3.100 | 2.350 | 5.532 | 58.500 | 1.907 | 2.050 | 1.592 | 2.602 | 0.134 | 25.530 | 50.540 | 8.200 |
| 9. | 178.000 | 2.600 | 1.000 | 20.250 | 10.120 | 70.000 | 1.939 | 0.0930 | 0.342 | 43.000 | 1.830 | 0.750 | 2.198 | 0.580 | 0.069 | 21.920 | 17.380 | 5.000 |
| 10. | 170.000 | 21.610 | 3.000 | 42.800 | 20.160 | 110.000 | 2.225 | 1.310 | 4.623 | 98.000 | 2.277 | 1.436 | 1.088 | 2.100 | 0.173 | 34.970 | 86.340 | 10.500 |
| 11. | 109.00 | 32.430 | 2.000 | 18.360 | 9.820 | 64.000 | 1.402 | 0.690 | 0.423 | 29.360 | 0.817 | 2.150 | 1.435 | 0.556 | 0.100 | 24.950 | 80.200 | 8.000 |
| 12. | 6.000 | 18.930 | 2.000 | 13.550 | 82.710 | 176.000 | 0.995 | 0.260 | 0.210 | 33.500 | 1.021 | 1.950 | 0.725 | 0.290 | 0.142 | 23.950 | 87.320 | 11.500 |
| 13. | 73.000 | 17.190 | 4.000 | 34.770 | 29.130 | 78.000 | 1.540 | 0.970 | 2.942 | 105.800 | 1.527 | 1.370 | 1.101 | 2.740 | 0.116 | 23.120 | 42.200 | 6.500 |
| 14. | 92.000 | 19.360 | 1.000 | 14.560 | 15.610 | 110.000 | 1.843 | 1.170 | 0.760 | 25.280 | 1.659 | 0.730 | 1.016 | 0.530 | 0.090 | 21.940 | 52.200 | 6.000 |
| 15. | 103.000 | 23.200 | 1.000 | 18.500 | 16.210 | 70.000 | 1.712 | 1.290 | 2.683 | 32.550 | 1.008 | 1.140 | 1.925 | 1.020 | 0.133 | 24.130 | 80.200 | 4.200 |
| 16. | 37.000 | 20.730 | 1.000 | 8.780 | 15.100 | 132.000 | 0.916 | 0.570 | 0.276 | 16.050 | 1.254 | 1.099 | 0.549 | 0.500 | 0.108 | 23.150 | 50.340 | 4.000 |
| 17. | 85.000 | 25.020 | 10.000 | 8.060 | 8.620 | 70.000 | 0.970 | 0.680 | 0.595 | 23.050 | 1.853 | 0.930 | 1.371 | 0.590 | 0.088 | 23.140 | 50.340 | 9.000 |

*cont...*

| | DP | SB | CA | DU | PD | D | ED | TP | ID | MF | WR | MECA | AGO | BAC | SMR | AA | LIV | AL |
|---|---|---|---|---|---|---|---|---|---|---|---|---|---|---|---|---|---|---|
| 18. | 106.000 | 41.820 | 2.000 | 17.900 | 15.810 | 77.000 | 1.171 | 0.920 | 0.425 | 43.600 | 1.992 | 1.600 | 2.011 | 0.700 | 0.171 | 23.930 | 64.340 | 5.000 |
| 19. | 125.000 | 9.280 | 2.000 | 14.390 | 47.620 | 72.000 | 1.607 | 0.910 | 1.991 | 26.500 | 2.438 | 0.800 | 3.115 | 0.610 | 0.128 | 24.720 | 117.340 | 6.200 |
| 20. | 136.000 | 34.330 | 4.000 | 15.050 | 39.620 | 93.000 | 2.385 | 1.840 | 2.391 | 57.566 | 2.212 | 0.910 | 2.254 | 0.710 | 0.105 | 23.870 | 130.340 | 5.000 |
| 21. | 114.000 | 16.610 | 2.000 | 13.180 | 27.620 | 71.000 | 1.687 | 0.860 | 1.195 | 33.000 | 2.148 | 1.390 | 2.595 | 0.580 | 0.140 | 23.730 | 96.320 | 7.500 |
| 22. | 181.000 | 64.440 | 2.000 | 64.000 | 9.620 | 77.000 | 1.500 | 0.730 | 0.571 | 53.560 | 2.318 | 1.060 | 2.128 | 0.810 | 0.204 | 21.400 | 110.320 | 6.500 |
| 23. | 176.000 | 72.630 | 2.000 | 6.220 | 15.210 | 93.000 | 1.330 | 0.700 | 0.279 | 26.560 | 2.165 | 0.490 | 1.927 | 0.300 | 0.079 | 22.730 | 116.200 | 6.200 |
| 24. | 106.000 | 39.020 | 2.000 | 17.010 | 26.620 | 60.000 | 1.497 | 0.0700 | 2.936 | 40.000 | 2.870 | 1.960 | 3.193 | 0.640 | 0.193 | 24.030 | 96.340 | 3.400 |
| 25. | 125.000 | 33.640 | 3.000 | 31.930 | 17.180 | 55.000 | 2.344 | 1.320 | 7.851 | 42.050 | 2.554 | 1.620 | 2.854 | 1.290 | 0.229 | 23.560 | 84.340 | 6.000 |
| 26. | 126.000 | 28.770 | 2.000 | 11.660 | 9.160 | 75.000 | 1.496 | 0.870 | 1.237 | 45.080 | 5.001 | 0.880 | 1.392 | 0.543 | 0.134 | 22.370 | 98.340 | 7.200 |

## APPENDIX - 2

**Percentage of Twelve Types of Migration Stream Based on Place of Birth and Place of Enumeration (males, 1971, 1981)**

INTRA-DISTRICT

| District | 1971 R-R | 1981 R-R | 1971 U-R | 1981 U-R | 1971 R-U | 1981 R-U | 1971 U-U | 1981 U-U |
|---|---|---|---|---|---|---|---|---|
| Sri Ganga-nagar | 78.85 | 77.28 | 6.75 | 6.81 | 9.47 | 9.62 | 4.93 | 6.24 |
| Bikaner | 59.24 | 57.95 | 9.32 | 10.74 | 25.79 | 23.32 | 5.65 | 7.99 |
| Churu | 53.58 | 53.30 | 11.63 | 13.60 | 20.98 | 22.64 | 13.81 | 10.46 |
| Jhunjhunu | 68.91 | 54.46 | 6.34 | 5.37 | 18.32 | 30.65 | 6.43 | 9.52 |
| Alwar | 70.27 | 65.23 | 4.58 | 4.76 | 22.47 | 25.36 | 2.68 | 4.65 |
| Bharatpur | 70.76 | 56.68 | 5.31 | 5.15 | 18.52 | 28.56 | 5.41 | 9.61 |
| Swai Madhopur | 69.32 | 58.69 | 4.44 | 7.25 | 21.51 | 28.16 | 4.77 | 5.91 |
| Jaipur | 53.04 | 44.51 | 5.40 | 5.25 | 34.95 | 39.86 | 6.52 | 10.38 |
| Sikar | 70.88 | 62.64 | 7.42 | 7.62 | 17.30 | 24.82 | 4.30 | 4.92 |
| Ajmer | 42.36 | 40.38 | 6.91 | 7.54 | 34.41 | 32.54 | 16.32 | 14.54 |
| Tonk | 68.30 | 62.72 | 10.45 | 8.34 | 16.31 | 23.76 | 4.94 | 5.18 |
| Jaisalmer | 69.68 | 71.15 | 5.44 | 6.60 | 23.49 | 20.72 | 1.39 | 1.53 |
| Jodhpur | 63.46 | 62.28 | 6.76 | 5.34 | 24.80 | 26.83 | 4.98 | 5.55 |
| Nagaur | 77.35 | 6.19 | 5.26 | 6.19 | 15.17 | 17.14 | 2.22 | 3.99 |
| Pali | 74.31 | 61.35 | 3.84 | 5.64 | 19.40 | 22.26 | 2.45 | 5.75 |
| Barmer | 78.82 | 69.67 | 4.37 | 3.88 | 15.96 | 25.53 | 0.85 | 0.92 |

INTER-DISTRICT

| District | 1971 R-R | 1981 R-R | 1971 U-R | 1981 U-R | 1971 R-U | 1981 R-U | 1971 U-U | 1981 U-U |
|---|---|---|---|---|---|---|---|---|
| Sri Ganga-nagar | 47.59 | 47.03 | 9.07 | 6.74 | 23.15 | 25.03 | 20.19 | 21.21 |
| Bikaner | 32.36 | 48.33 | 7.84 | 6.54 | 32.94 | 26.51 | 26.86 | 18.62 |
| Churu | 42.62 | 43.87 | 8.67 | 8.52 | 20.97 | 21.28 | 27.74 | 26.33 |
| Jhunjhunu | 44.11 | 39.28 | 15.26 | 13.29 | 15.24 | 22.64 | 25.39 | 24.74 |
| Alwar | 31.37 | 46.57 | 8.09 | 11.21 | 28.77 | 22.92 | 31.77 | 19.30 |
| Bharatpur | 55.26 | 39.26 | 9.51 | 7.88 | 16.91 | 26.38 | 18.32 | 26.48 |
| Swai Madhopur | 42.61 | 39.03 | 11.23 | 9.38 | 20.34 | 24.80 | 25.81 | 26.79 |
| Jaipur | 17.19 | 14.44 | 3.48 | 2.57 | 33.57 | 42.37 | 44.76 | 40.62 |
| Sikar | 56.43 | 49.53 | 11.44 | 10.44 | 13.18 | 20.28 | 18.45 | 19.75 |
| Ajmer | 20.33 | 19.88 | 4.32 | 3.83 | 44.46 | 47.84 | 30.79 | 28.45 |
| Tonk | 54.33 | 47.82 | 14.25 | 11.79 | 15.77 | 19.14 | 15.65 | 23.25 |
| Jaisalmer | 38.86 | 66.47 | 5.05 | 12.64 | 32.12 | 12.32 | 23.47 | 12.32 |
| Jodhpur | 24.67 | 23.58 | 0.001 | 3.63 | 38.35 | 42.98 | 32.33 | 29.81 |
| Nagaur | 46.68 | 49.37 | 16.62 | 19.26 | 14.15 | 11.92 | 22.55 | 19.45 |
| Pali | 42.67 | 34.52 | 16.66 | 11.91 | 18.74 | 24.30 | 21.93 | 29.07 |
| Barmer | 49.22 | 52.57 | 13.75 | 8.87 | 21.65 | 19.59 | 15.38 | 18.97 |

INTER-STATE

| District | 1971 R-R | 1981 R-R | 1971 U-R | 1981 U-R | 1971 R-U | 1981 R-U | 1971 U-U | 1981 U-U |
|---|---|---|---|---|---|---|---|---|
| Sri Ganga-nagar | 67.86 | 65.53 | 5.22 | 4.82 | 16.97 | 19.93 | 9.95 | 11.72 |
| Bikaner | 12.59 | 23.28 | 5.68 | 6.53 | 39.79 | 34.39 | 41.94 | 35.80 |
| Churu | 42.24 | 40.38 | 4.29 | 5.75 | 19.21 | 21.64 | 34.26 | 32.23 |
| Jhunjhunu | 30.53 | 31.46 | 18.96 | 11.58 | 13.87 | 24.52 | 36.64 | 32.44 |
| Alwar | 60.42 | 55.57 | 12.98 | 10.32 | 13.85 | 14.96 | 12.75 | 19.15 |
| Bharatpur | 52.82 | 41.33 | 0.28 | 8.57 | 16.49 | 29.66 | 30.41 | 20.49 |
| Swai Madhopur | 20.21 | 21.81 | 15.42 | 12.84 | 30.62 | 26.54 | 30.41 | 20.49 |
| Jaipur | 3.79 | 5.43 | 5.81 | 5.34 | 33.59 | 29.28 | 56.81 | 59.95 |
| Sikar | 33.25 | 24.13 | 18.86 | 22.15 | 11.59 | 15.88 | 36.30 | 37.84 |
| Ajmer | 3.45 | 2.24 | 2.94 | 3.83 | 36.99 | 42.57 | 56.62 | 51.36 |
| Tonk | 12.89 | 20.01 | 14.06 | 27.76 | 42.77 | 17.68 | 26.38 | 34.55 |
| Jaisalmer | 8.16 | 8.38 | 4.90 | 6.36 | 53.06 | 29.69 | 33.85 | 55.57 |
| Jodhpur | 4.09 | 5.95 | 3.07 | 4.61 | 22.47 | 27.57 | 70.37 | 61.87 |
| Nagaur | 27.70 | 29.26 | 24.05 | 26.99 | 18.45 | 14.51 | 29.80 | 29.24 |
| Pali | 22.31 | 18.24 | 43.58 | 28.45 | 11.98 | 15.95 | 22.13 | 37.36 |
| Barmer | 27.22 | 29.34 | 20.42 | 15.96 | 31.29 | 20.23 | 21.07 | 34.47 |

*cont...*

| District | 1971 R-R | 1981 R-R | 1971 U-R | 1981 U-R | 1971 R-U | 1981 R-U | 1971 U-U | 1981 U-U | 1971 R-R | 1981 R-R | 1971 U-R | 1981 U-R | 1971 R-U | 1981 R-U | 1971 U-U | 1981 U-U | 1971 R-R | 1981 R-R | 1971 U-R | 1981 U-R | 1971 R-U | 1981 R-U | 1971 U-U | 1981 U-U |
|---|---|---|---|---|---|---|---|---|---|---|---|---|---|---|---|---|---|---|---|---|---|---|---|---|
| Jalore | 84.43 | 77.15 | 5.63 | 3.96 | 9.06 | 17.97 | 0.85 | 0.92 | 65.57 | 55.94 | 13.88 | 11.92 | 10.68 | 24.52 | 9.87 | 7.60 | 45.52 | 37.82 | 44.37 | 34.27 | 4.84 | 11.99 | 5.27 | 15.92 |
| Sirohi | 71.89 | 71.25 | 7.79 | 8.69 | 16.19 | 14.33 | 4.13 | 5.73 | 36.93 | 39.38 | 6.92 | 6.53 | 23.18 | 25.48 | 32.97 | 28.30 | 29.82 | 24.96 | 12.14 | 8.78 | 16.83 | 17.57 | 41.21 | 38.69 |
| Bhilwara | 78.78 | 66.47 | 2.77 | 4.57 | 16.16 | 24.72 | 2.29 | 4.14 | 47.59 | 45.63 | 9.96 | 11.98 | 19.03 | 23.85 | 23.40 | 18.54 | 23.95 | 48.06 | 18.25 | 37.63 | 16.66 | 7.06 | 41.14 | 7.25 |
| Udaipur | 69.31 | 63.61 | 9.82 | 7.88 | 15.92 | 22.66 | 4.96 | 5.85 | 38.73 | 38.53 | 10.65 | 8.65 | 19.76 | 25.89 | 30.86 | 26.91 | 32.56 | 29.86 | 17.82 | 18.56 | 13.20 | 18.10 | 36.42 | 33.48 |
| Chittor | 78.76 | 74.49 | 7.67 | 5.52 | 10.45 | 16.32 | 2.62 | 3.67 | 61.28 | 57.23 | 12.36 | 9.47 | 13.48 | 18.76 | 12.76 | 14.54 | 55.13 | 50.15 | 19.96 | 11.74 | 8.36 | 17.50 | 16.55 | 20.61 |
| Dungarpur | 94.75 | 87.13 | 1.19 | 3.31 | 3.78 | 8.78 | 0.28 | 0.78 | 44.45 | 43.92 | 10.98 | 7.87 | 19.79 | 24.39 | 24.78 | 23.87 | 42.52 | 42.76 | 20.27 | 17.65 | 15.35 | 17.95 | 21.86 | 21.65 |
| Banswara | 80.41 | 87.83 | 4.56 | 3.31 | 13.22 | 7.68 | 1.81 | 0.66 | 47.39 | 48.72 | 17.99 | 15.01 | 14.79 | 18.34 | 19.83 | 17.83 | 55.82 | 47.72 | 12.62 | 16.77 | 10.71 | 18.74 | 20.85 | 16.77 |
| Bundi | 81.22 | 68.55 | 5.64 | 9.56 | 11.32 | 18.55 | 1.82 | 3.34 | 64.36 | 59.88 | 12.09 | 12.16 | 12.89 | 16.27 | 10.66 | 11.69 | 57.67 | 59.20 | 19.94 | 17.17 | 10.97 | 13.68 | 11.42 | 9.95 |
| Kota | 70.68 | 56.57 | 5.22 | 5.45 | 20.35 | 30.53 | 3.75 | 7.45 | 32.05 | 31.94 | 4.97 | 5.87 | 3210 | 33.23 | 30.88 | 26.96 | 24.59 | 28.20 | 6.47 | 4.21 | 32.50 | 330.73 | 3636 | 36.86 |
| Jhalawar | 78.51 | 70.86 | 5.84 | 4.92 | 11.83 | 18.42 | 3.82 | 5.80 | 49.13 | 47.73 | 9.88 | 10.93 | 20.11 | 23.85 | 20.88 | 17.48 | 64.87 | 62.49 | 12.72 | 9.28 | 9.92 | 13.79 | 12.49 | 14.44 |
| Rajasthan | 71.22 | 84.26 | 5.83 | 6.23 | 18.69 | 23.23 | 4.36 | 6.39 | 39.58 | 38.65 | 8.96 | 24.92 | 28.72 | 28.72 | 26.35 | 7.74 | 41.14 | 38.85 | 9.69 | 29.09 | 21.63 | 23.65 | 27.54 | 8.39 |

## APPENDIX - 3

### Zero-order Correlation Matrix for Explanatory Variables, 1971

| | DP | SB | CA | DU | PD | D | ED | TP | ID | MF | WR | MECA | AGO | BAC | SMR | AA | LIV | AL |
|---|---|---|---|---|---|---|---|---|---|---|---|---|---|---|---|---|---|---|
| DP | 1.00000 | | | | | | | | | | | | | | | | | |
| SB | .23677 | 1.00000 | | | | | | | | | | | | | | | | |
| CA | .25627 | .11358 | 1.00000 | | | | | | | | | | | | | | | |
| DU | -.12828 | -.33734 | .47967 | 1.00000 | | | | | | | | | | | | | | |
| PD | -.42903 | -.16264 | .37276 | -.45334 | 1.00000 | | | | | | | | | | | | | |
| D | -.34721 | -.28333 | .03752 | .04902 | .50414 | 1.00000 | | | | | | | | | | | | |
| ED | .62018 | -.12141 | .44094 | .40380 | .08745 | -.04800 | 1.00000 | | | | | | | | | | | |
| TP | .45201 | -.18788 | .05634 | .33112 | -.27862 | -.10276 | .48128 | 1.00000 | | | | | | | | | | |
| ID | .14389 | .04495 | .42588 | .54477 | .31908 | -.16159 | .51037 | .45313 | 1.00000 | | | | | | | | | |
| MF | -.10133 | -.13765 | .69239 | .77855 | .49450 | .16328 | .23412 | .11280 | .30085 | 1.00000 | | | | | | | | |
| WR | .04092 | .04270 | -.00472 | -0.9402 | -.14926 | -0.3627 | -0.8582 | .06827 | .00542 | -0.3094 | 1.00000 | | | | | | | |
| MECA | -.23959 | -.14773 | -.25822 | .25367 | .15164 | .30474 | .10945 | -0.3779 | .01037 | -.13591 | -.06421 | 1.00000 | | | | | | |
| AGO | .27040 | .14287 | .10905 | -.31117 | -.25637 | -.10144 | .16625 | .13613 | .12757 | -.33841 | .22886 | .17510 | 1.00000 | | | | | |
| BAC | .49750 | -.08103 | .46303 | .29711 | .06196 | .01272 | .78887 | .47719 | .55179 | .04155 | -.08544 | .27473 | .42758 | 1.00000 | | | | |
| SMR | -.13249 | -.02901 | -.21530 | .03282 | .27509 | .55654 | .17542 | -.01928 | .02096 | -.10947 | -.03969 | .72890 | .16989 | .18126 | -1.00000 | 1.00000 | | |
| AA | .14120 | -.12313 | .15091 | .33377 | -.05410 | -.07972 | .34643 | .44470 | .28508 | .17343 | -.00987 | -.01845 | -.06046 | .14614 | -.03059 | 1.00000 | | |
| LIV | .13963 | .51400 | .17962 | -.33776 | 0.3827 | -.17872 | -.22315 | -.49610 | -.10555 | -.06142 | -.01975 | -.37911 | .09503 | -.32589 | -.23911 | .02754 | 1.00000 | |
| AL | .10120 | -0.1382 | .04973 | -.00034 | .06548 | .25040 | .13581 | .21501 | .08268 | -.10551 | -.14569 | .12089 | -.00967 | .17744 | .16533 | .486838 | .07508 | 1.00000 |

Critical Value (1-Tail, .051 *+ Dr -.33020

Critical Value (2-Tail, .051 * +/- .38743

## APPENDIX - 4

**Zero-order Correlation Matrix for Explanatory Variables, 1981**

| | *DP* | *SB* | *CA* | *DU* | *PD* | *D* | *ED* | *TP* | *ID* | *MF* | *WR* | *MECA* | *AGO* | *BAC* | *SMR* | *AA* | *LIV* | *AL* |
|---|---|---|---|---|---|---|---|---|---|---|---|---|---|---|---|---|---|---|
| DP | 1.00000 | | | | | | | | | | | | | | | | | |
| SB | -0.5372 | 1.00000 | | | | | | | | | | | | | | | | |
| CA | .18601 | -.06673 | 1.00000 | | | | | | | | | | | | | | | |
| DU | -.32648 | .07088 | .34169 | 1.00000 | | | | | | | | | | | | | | |
| PD | -.38756 | -.16203 | .50232 | .03679 | 1.00000 | | | | | | | | | | | | | |
| D | -.32454 | -.11551 | .47121 | -.03448 | .65485 | 1.00000 | | | | | | | | | | | | |
| ED | .74429 | -.34269 | .52911 | .31153 | .07761 | -.03469 | 1.00000 | | | | | | | | | | | |
| TP | -.14197 | -.09085 | .29646 | .25766 | -.61953 | -.24724 | .11138 | 1.00000 | | | | | | | | | | |
| ID | .22714 | .10175 | .52257 | .29113 | .09327 | -.07526 | .62620 | .01030 | 1.00000 | | | | | | | | | |
| MF | .00432 | -.08409 | .50399 | .57583 | .46526 | .12365 | .10417 | .73813 | .26156 | 1.00000 | | | | | | | | |
| WR | .37303 | .13546 | -.05191 | -.02309 | -.35167 | -.39403 | .17796 | -.21269 | .14063 | -.06333 | 1.00000 | | | | | | | |
| MECA | -.13125 | -.04225 | .57800 | .05815 | .35519 | .62025 | .17888 | -.02961 | .19291 | -.07777 | -.25653 | 1.00000 | | | | | | |
| AGO | .40067 | .01843 | .28136 | -.00794 | -.10758 | -.09930 | .41865 | -.27114 | .26952 | -.34591 | .24517 | .36816 | 1.00000 | | | | | |
| BAC | .03281 | -.13635 | .60767 | .47536 | .34512 | .15683 | .33123 | .34396 | .61046 | .66875 | -.20863 | .29189 | .21452 | 1.00000 | | | | |
| SMR | -.22027 | .26164 | -.50948 | .30278 | .38056 | .43346 | .06705 | .08156 | .041981 | .12780 | -.04561 | .77715 | .33652 | .38756 | 1.00000 | | | |
| AA | .19891 | -.13777 | .18537 | .18675 | .03418 | .05777 | .29185 | -.07947 | .40785 | .26213 | .00142 | .06294 | -.09473 | .35927 | .12406 | 1.00000 | | |
| LIV | .12370 | .53164 | .03560 | -.03190 | .06343 | -.17509 | -.01015 | -.11947 | -.04045 | -.03845 | -.39645 | -.23498 | .20353 | -.28510 | .08917 | .16754 | 1.00000 | |
| AL | .02587 | -.11628 | .16865 | .03366 | .09357 | .33757 | 11275 | -.36510 | .06534 | -.16347 | -.03873 | .31570 | -.07221 | .07632 | .13554 | .43158 | -.03319 | 1.00000 |

## APPENDIX - 5

### Zero-order Correlation Matrix for Ratios of Explanatory Variables, 1971

| | DP | SB | CA | DU | PD | D | ED | TP | ID | MF | WR | MECA | AGO | BAC | SMR | AA | LIV | AL | |
|---|---|---|---|---|---|---|---|---|---|---|---|---|---|---|---|---|---|---|---|
| DP | 1.00000 | | | | | | | | | | | | | | | | | | |
| SB | .17542 | 1.00000 | | | | | | | | | | | | | | | | | |
| CA | .13354 | -.12127 | 1.00000 | | | | | | | | | | | | | | | | |
| DU | -.05374 | .23879 | .24704 | 1.00000 | | | | | | | | | | | | | | | |
| PD | -.14007 | -.11723 | .10021 | .47563 | 1.00000 | | | | | | | | | | | | | | |
| ED | .11891 | -.16803 | .30187 | .37581 | .07422 | 1.00000 | | | | | | | | | | | | | |
| TP | .69023 | -.09427 | .29022 | .23660 | -.11299 | -.21433 | 1.00000 | | | | | | | | | | | | |
| ID | .16780 | .08394 | .25836 | .48927 | -.35882 | -.24869 | .48727 | 1.00000 | | | | | | | | | | | |
| MF | -.01159 | .08755 | .26613 | .63378 | .41133 | -.41473 | .14246 | .26409 | 1.00000 | | | | | | | | | | |
| WR | .24074 | -.18925 | .02543 | .23990 | .01740 | .08755 | .52982 | .33542 | .09109 | 1.00000 | | | | | | | | | |
| MECA | -.08003 | .01092 | -.01628 | -.22103 | -.21576 | -.04274 | .04657 | .14144 | .00192 | -.08579 | 1.00000 | | | | | | | | |
| AGO | .45320 | .37973 | -.06617 | -.29536 | -.13373 | .01040 | .37517 | .07982 | -.17957 | .13908 | -.01752 | 1.00000 | | | | | | | |
| BAC | .53013 | -.01041 | .38124 | .23582 | .16398 | .29834 | .67069 | .57524 | .08253 | .18885 | .13493 | .33713 | 1.00000 | | | | | | |
| SMR | .07647 | .33622 | -.11562 | .08278 | .30044 | .00127 | .12682 | .34982 | .09904 | .33001 | .40598 | .23857 | .21055 | 1.00000 | | | | | |
| AA | .05045 | -.10613 | .07850 | .36138 | .12492 | .06419 | .41933 | .41133 | .25095 | .49505 | .09213 | .10123 | .18984 | .23064 | 1.00000 | | | | |
| LIV | .04940 | .45636 | -.18988 | -.26708 | .04295 | -.21972 | -.15473 | -.08333 | .00379 | -.02247 | -.19833 | .23159 | -.21553 | .07801 | .14882 | 1.00000 | | | |
| AL | .04171 | .07172 | -.04249 | -.08509 | -.00641 | .03493 | .03654 | -.00591 | -.10811 | -.02735 | .11868 | .30092 | .12256 | .06737 | .36649 | .04068 | 1.00000 | | |
| D | .13273 | .04331 | -.05834 | .00586 | .04727 | -.03345 | .06705 | .00964 | -.03500 | .01255 | .10862 | .08746 | .10025 | .01915 | -.00141 | .09674 | -.02319 | 1.00000 | |
| DV | .28354 | .19268 | .07933 | -.22333 | -.17890 | -.02353 | .11788 | -.14959 | -.11250 | -.10949 | -.08138 | .25868 | .06913 | -.07562 | -.19260 | -.03530 | .18776 | -.02578 | 1.00000 |

Critical Value (1-Tail, .051 * + Dr - .06459

Critical Value (2-Tail, .051 * +/- .07692

## APPENDIX - 6

### Zero-order Correlation Matrix for the Ratios of Explanatory Variables, 1981

| | *DP* | *SB* | *CA* | *DU* | *PD* | *D* | *ED* | *TP* | *ID* | *MF* | *WR* | *MECA* | *AGO* | *BAC* | *SMR* | *AA* | *LIV* | *AL* | |
|---|---|---|---|---|---|---|---|---|---|---|---|---|---|---|---|---|---|---|---|
| DP | 1.00000 | | | | | | | | | | | | | | | | | | |
| SB | -.06180 | 1.00000 | | | | | | | | | | | | | | | | | |
| CA | .03869 | .02016 | 1.00000 | | | | | | | | | | | | | | | | |
| DU | .11832 | -.04968 | .30238 | 1.00000 | | | | | | | | | | | | | | | |
| PD | -.16443 | -.02967 | .46853 | .04539 | 1.00000 | | | | | | | | | | | | | | |
| ED | .42839 | -.27093 | .44770 | .38736 | .02491 | 1.00000 | | | | | | | | | | | | | |
| TP | .05272 | -.04275 | .19654 | .19699 | .41266 | -.01413 | 1.00000 | | | | | | | | | | | | |
| ID | .34902 | -.01410 | .42615 | .30632 | .11960 | .56853 | .06192 | 1.00000 | | | | | | | | | | | |
| MF | .01562 | -.06376 | .41358 | .52406 | .31507 | .15719 | .52801 | .19474 | 1.00000 | | | | | | | | | | |
| WR | .29374 | -.02392 | .01268 | -.03615 | -.23722 | .23858 | -.10954 | .17253 | .00397 | 1.00000 | | | | | | | | | |
| MECA | -.07673 | -.01440 | .47496 | .19993 | .30565 | .15523 | -.02312 | .17935 | .00086 | -.25202 | 1.00000 | | | | | | | | |
| AGO | .39431 | -.10553 | .25513 | .05675 | -.06814 | .49613 | -.11956 | .30748 | -.17051 | .31236 | .19418 | 1.00000 | | | | | | | |
| BAC | .07507 | .04650 | .12736 | .13329 | .20691 | .06152 | .14927 | .23646 | .21710 | -.12414 | .08250 | -.12989 | 1.00000 | | | | | | |
| SMR | -.07745 | .30115 | .49904 | .31510 | .37241 | .05484 | .05748 | .35091 | .18142 | -.05973 | .69000 | .17883 | .21136 | 1.00000 | | | | | |
| AA | .03345 | .01001 | .20906 | .17591 | .11647 | .26961 | -.04661 | .28882 | .20873 | -.00005 | .12755 | -.04774 | .16966 | .16325 | 1.00000 | | | | |
| LIV | -.05491 | .55838 | .20041 | -.09132 | .12466 | -.03703 | -.06320 | .07875 | .00601 | .22652 | -.07206 | .09802 | -.11593 | .23232 | .20949 | 1.00000 | | | |
| AL | -.16056 | -.03366 | .20571 | .06023 | .02777 | .09414 | -.22421 | .00760 | -.06172 | -.04703 | .20376 | -.05840 | -.03114- | .04790 | .32543 | .03579 | 1.00000 | | |
| D | .12954 | .05023 | -.03328 | -.00103 | .02954 | .04436 | .00098 | .02378 | -.04343 | .02029 | .07409 | .08798 | -.00162 | .03214 | -.00361 | .04959 | -.00928 | 1.00000 | |
| DV | .26442 | -.12627 | -.03272 | -.12542 | -.19138 | .07869 | .01769 | -.05912 | -.13260 | .30016 | -.04969 | .23302 | -.11350 | -.12287 | -.20080 | -.14985 | .03092 | -.02429 | 1.00000 |

# *Bibliography*

Agarwala, S.N.(1958): "Method for estimating decade internal migration in cities from Indian Census Data", *Indian Economic Review,* Feb., No. 4.

Agarwala, S.N.(1968): "Socio-economic and demographic characteristic of the rural migrants and non-migrants", *Journal of the Institute of Economic Research,* July No. 3.

Amrit Lal (1961): "Patterns of Inmigration in Indian cities", *Geographical Review of India,* Sept., No. 23.

Banerjee, Biswajit (1974): *Migration Theory and Evidence including some discussion of migration to Delhi.* Unpublished B. Phil. thesis submitted at the University of Oxford.

Banerjee, Biswajit: "Some methodological aspects of analysis of data on internal migration". *Paper contributed to Third Seminar on Data Base of Indian Economy, New Delhi.*

Banerjee, Biswajit (1983): "The Role of the Informal Sector in the Migration Process: A Test of Probabilistic Migration Models and Labour Market Segmentation for India", *Oxford Economic Papers,* Vol. 35, No. 3, Nov.

Barter, A.P. (1974): "The Migration Decision: What Role Does Job Mobility Play?" *American Economic Review,* Vol. 69, No. 5.

Bogue, D.J. (1952): "Internal Migration", *American Sociologic Review,* Vol. XIV, 2.

Bhargava, G. (1968): Impact of Rural Migration on Urban areas in India". *Khadi Gramodyog,* July, No. 14.

Bhasakara Rao, N. (1965): *Estimate of Migration to Metropolitan Cities of India 1941-51 and 1951-61"* Bombay Demographic Training & Research Centre 26, (mimeo).

Bose, Ashish (1965): "Internal Migration in India, Pakistan & Ceylon, in Registrar General", India. *Papers contributed by Indian authors to the World Population Conference*, Belgrade, 1965, New Delhi, 1965.

Bose, Ashish (1965): "Why do people migrate to cities?", Yojana, Vol. 30, Jan No. 26.

Bose, Ashish (1965): "Migration streams in India" *Paper presented to International Union for the Scientific Study of Population, Sydney Conference.*

Beals, R.E., M.B. Levy & L.N. Moses (1967): "Rationality and Migration in Ghana". *The Review of Economics & Statistics,* Vol. X, No. 49.

Blanco, C. (1964): "Prospective Unemployment & Internal Population Movement." *The Review of Economics & Statistics,* No. 46.

Chakrabarty, B. (1974): "Development of Internal migration data in India and possibility of its use in city and regional planning". *Paper contributed to the Third Seminar on Data Base of Indian Economic,* New Delhi.

Chatterjee, Atrevi & Bose, Ashish (1974): "Demographic data on internal migration and urbanization from census and N.S.S."—*a critical appraisal contributed to Third Seminar on Data Base of Indian Economy,* New Delhi.

Caldwell, J.C. (1968): "Determinants of Rural-Urban Migration in Ghana"; *Population Studies,* Vol. 2 No. 22.

Dasgupta, B. and Roy Laishley (1975): "Migration from Villages", *Economic and Political Weekly,* Vol. X, No. 42.

Dunbby, J.A. and N.A. Gemery (1977): "The Role of Migrant Stock and Lagged Migration in the Settlement patterns of nineteenth century In-migrants"; *The Review of Economics and Statistics,* No. 2.

Dayal, P. (1959): "Population growth and rural-urban migration in India". *National Geographical Journal of India,* Dec., Vol. 5.

Davis Kingsley (1954): "Internal Migration and Urbanization in Relation to Economic Development", *World Population Conference,* Vol. II.

ECAFE Secretariat (1967): "Internal Migration, Urbanization and Settlement". *Paper prepared for ECAFE Expert Working Group on Internal Migration and Urbanisation,* Bangkok.

ECAFE Secretariat (1967): "Statistics on Internal Migration". *Paper prepared for ECAFE Expert Working Group on Internal Migration and Urbanisation,* Bangkok.

Fabricant, Ruth (1970): "An Expectational Model of Migration", *Jr. of Regional Science,* Vol. 10, April No. 1.

Fields, G.S. (1979): "Place to Place Migration: Some new evidence", *The Review of Economics and Statistics,* Vol. LXI, Feb. No. 1.

Fogarty, T. and D. Mehta (1984): "On the micro-economics of Rural to Urban Migration: A Conceptual framework and some Empirical observations, " *Indian Journal of Regional Science,* Vol. XVI, No. 2.

Ghosh, Ambica (1965): "Inmigration from Rural areas in to Calcutta Metropolitan Region; analysis and projections in Registrar General, India". *Papers contributed by Indian Authors to the World Population Conference,* Belgrade.

Ghosh, Ambica (1967): "A Note on internal migration and urbanization". *Paper prepared for ECAFE Expert Working Group on Internal Migration and Urbanization,* Bangkok.

Greenwood, M.J. (1969): "An analysis of the Determinants of Geographical Labour Mobility in the U.S.A". *Review of Economic & Statistics,* No. 16.

Greenwood, M.J. (1969): "Lagged Response in the Decision to Migrate". *Jr. of Regional Science,* Vol. 10, No. 3.

Greenwood, M.J. (1969): "Determinants of Internal Migration" *Demography,* Vol. 9, Feb., No. 7.

Greenwood, M.J. (1969): "The Determinants of Labour Migration in Egypt". *Journal of Regional Sciences,* Vol. XI, No. 9.

Greenwood, M.J. (1969): "A Regression Analysis of Migration to Urban Areas of less developed country: The case of India". *Journal of Regional Science,* Vol. XI, No. 20.

Gupta, P.Sen (1967): "Some characteristics of internal migration in India". *Paper prepared for ECAFE Expert Working Group on Internal Migration and Urbanization,* Bangkok.

Gaude, J. (1976): "Causes and Repercussions of Rural Migration in Developing Countries: A critical analysis", *I.L.O. World Employment Programme Working Paper,* WEP/10-6/WP 10: Oct.

Gumber, A.K. (1983): "Sectoral Level of Development and Migration in Gujarat: A District Level Analysis", *anvesak,* Vol. XIII, June, No. 1.

Gupta, S.K. (1989): "Inter-state Migration and National Integration", *The Journal of Sociological Studies,* Vol. 8, Jan.

Hart, R.A. (1975): "International Economic Migration: Some Theoretical Considerations (Part I & II)". *Journal of Regional Science,* Vol. X, No. 15.

Hannan, D.P. (1970): "Migration Motives & Migration Differentials among fresh rural youth". *Sociological Abstract,* No. 7.

Hannan and Young (1977): "Estimation in Panel Models: Results on Pooling cross sections and Time Series", Chap.2, in David K. Heise (eds), *Sociological Methodology,* San Francisco, Jossey-Bass.

Hay, M.J. (1980): "A Structural Equations Model of Migration in Tunisia", *Economic Development and Cultural Change,* Vol. 28, Jan, No. 2.

Harris, J. and M.P. Todaro (1970): "Migration, Unemployment and Development: A Two Sector Analysis", *American Economic Review.*

I.L.O. (1982): "World Employment Programme," *Population and Development,* 4th ed.

Suar, Damodar (1984): "Development Indicator Identification and Regional Disparity in Orissa—A factor Analysis Study", *Indian Journal of Regional Science,* Vol. XVI, No. 2.

Todaro, M.P. (1976): "Internal Migration in Developing Countries: A Review of Theory, Evidence, Methodology and Research Priorities", *I.L.O.* Geneva.

Todaro, M.P. (1969): "A Model of Labour Migration and Urban Unemployment in Less Developed Countries", *American Economic Review,* Vol. VIX, March, No. 1.

United Nations (1984): *Internal Migration in Asia and the Pacific,* ESCAP, No. 4.

United Nations (1985): *Urbanization in Asia and the Pacific,* ESCAP, No. 5.

Zachariah, K.C. (1960): *Internal Migration in India 1941-1951,* Bombay, Demographic Research Centre.

Zachariah, K.C. (1965): *Method of Estimating Urban-ward Migration in India: With Application to Bihar, Bombay,* Demographic Research Training and Research Centre.

Zachariah, K.C. (1967): "Estimation of Return Migration from place of birth and duration of residence data". *Paper presented to International Union for the Scientific Study of Population, Sydnye Conference.*

Zachariah, K.C. (1968): *Migrants in Greater Bombay,* D.T.R.C. monograph 5.

Zachariah, K.C. (1964): *A Historical Study of Internal Migration in the Indian sub-continent, 1901-1931,* Ph.D. Thesis, Asia Publishing House, Bombay.

# Index

**N**



**O**



**P**



**R**



**S**



**T**



**Y**



**Z**